It's Only
a Game
×

It's Only a Game x

The Autobiography of
MISS WHIPLASH

Lindi St. Clair

WITH PAMELA WINFIELD

PIATKUS

In loving memory of my dear friends and
colleagues who have died of AIDS, at the
hands of brutal pimps and psychopathic
clients, and who have had no protection
under British law during the course of
their prostitution profession. God bless
them all.

© 1992 by Lindi St Clair and Pamela Winfield

First published in 1992 by
Judy Piatkus (Publishers) Ltd of
5 Windmill Street, London W1P 1HF

The moral right of the author
has been asserted

A catalogue record for this book is
available from the British Library

ISBN 0–7499–1171–9

Edited by Susan Fleming

Set in Linotron Sabon by
Phoenix Photosetting, Chatham, Kent
Printed and bound in Great Britain by
Butler & Tanner Ltd, Frome

*To all my special
darlings — you know
who you are . . .*

Acknowledgements

I would like to thank Judy Piatkus, Gill Cormode, Philip Cotterell and their team for giving me the opportunity to tell my story to the world.

Also, I would like to thank my co-writer Pamela Winfield and my agent Jane Conway-Gordon.

Lastly, I would like to thank libel lawyers Bronwen and Brian for leaving this book with a few lines from the original manuscript.

Contents

1

Childhood Adventures

I used to practise astral projection when I was about nine or ten. I'd sit in front of a mirror with a candle burning, concentrate on hyping myself up, and wait for my spirit to float out of the window. I was looking for excitement, but astral projection didn't seem to work.

I had more luck with Henry, the ghost of a young boy who had died on the land where our house was built. He was a mischievous poltergeist and did silly things, but he was always friendly. I'd get the blame. Once he put a vinegar bottle out on our doorstep; another time he put my mother's purse on top of the wardrobe. She didn't believe me when I said I hadn't done it, until something happened when I wasn't there. He followed me when I left and I still know when he's around because of a distinctive odour in the room. In fact, fifteen years later, when I was on a cruise, he'd been in my cabin, taken the tap apart and left it in the sink. Naturally, at first, I blamed the steward. He denied it. Not long after that, I was arguing with someone and Henry pushed her down the stairs.

I was the youngest in my family by three years. I had a sister and two brothers who were older. My sister and I had fights. We each had our own bedroom, and she kept hers locked because I was going through her clothes all the time. We hated each other, partly because I was always competing with her for our Dad. I was a Rocker, she was a Mod and his favourite. He said she took after his side of the family, while I took after my mother's. I was always trying to get his attention; I'd write him poems. My sister and I would squabble over who would cook his lunch; I did fried eggs on toast.

My brothers were above all this, too busy with trains and football to pay much attention, until their friends began to notice I was developing tits. They came to our house and ogled me. They'd ask me to let them 'tit me up' which meant standing behind me, arms round, feeling a tit in each hand. My brothers thought it was hilarious, and it made them popular with their friends.

My parents had a friend called Walter. He would let me sit on his knee. I was probably only five then. One night, after I'd gone to bed, he came upstairs, supposedly to the toilet, but he sneaked into my room. I was curious to see what was going to happen so I pretended to be asleep. He kissed me, all wet and sloppy. I didn't like that much, but I didn't move. He pulled back the covers, and slid his hand past my chest which obviously hadn't yet developed. Down in my pyjama trousers, he began to play around between my legs, feeling my fanny and my bum. I didn't dislike it or I would have screamed. I could hear a sort of rustling of clothes. I thought, what's he doing. . . . Of course, he was wanking himself off with the other hand.

I never told anyone about it. It was my special secret and I enjoyed having a secret that was all mine. To be honest, I think now that I looked forward to it. I was always looking for affection and attention. This situation went on for some time, me pretending to be asleep, him messing about with me – the first of the countless games I was to play from then on. The next day he'd give me coins from his jacket pocket, usually a couple of sixpences and several pennies. I spent this on Mars Bars and Sherbet Dabs. Then he moved away. That may have been the end of his sly paedophilia but it was the beginning of my enthusiasm for sexual experiences.

My parents had married against the wishes of both their families. My Mum was middle class, my Dad lower class. They moved to Wiltshire so there were no uncles, aunts or cousins around. We saw some on holidays, but even then my sister and I went our separate ways; she to my father's relations, me to my Mum's, so I've a lot of cousins on the other side who are still strangers to me. One of the aunts I visited lived with her husband in a big, rambling, Victorian house in the London suburbs. They had been in the furniture removal business for years, originally using horses and carts. The old stables were a store for furniture, and I loved to rummage around in there. I've always been incredibly nosey.

At home we all ate together except for Mum. We weren't allowed to talk. It was always the same for dinner: Fray Bentos steamed steak and kidney pudding, tinned peas, boiled potatoes and gravy. Mum ate in the kitchen; no one could go in while she was eating. She'd have boiled bacon sandwiches piled high; she was greedy. I must get both my greediness and fatness from her.

Although we never wanted for material things, none of us got many kisses or cuddles. (In fact, talking to my mother many years later, I discovered that both she and my father were brought up in much the same way. They were both loners, so to them it was the norm.)

To replace what I saw as a lack of love and affection at home, I clutched at anything that was devious, naughty or forbidden. I used to rifle through my mother's jewellery box when she was out, and pinch her diamond engagement and eternity rings to show off at school. I never lost them, but can you imagine if I had?

I cultivated friends at school by being the Number One Dude in the playground. I'd buy five packets of potato puffs or sweets, and dole them out. This brought plenty of hangers-on who wanted to be my best friend. My two real best friends were Susan, whose father ran a fish and chip shop where I satisfied my greediness for chips, and Juliet. She lived in a large detached house in the posh part of town. I stayed over at her house frequently. She was an only child, so her parents were glad to have me there. They even paid for me to go on holiday with them.

I truanted a lot from school. There was probably about a year when I hardly went to lessons. Everyone would cover for me, the boys in particular. All I had to do to get round them was let them look up my skirt or feel my tits. By now, I was developing faster than the rest of the girls. We'd muck about on the waste ground near the school where they were laying enormous pipes. Each section looked like a giant polo mint. We could duck down inside for privacy. I'd wanted to do 'it' for some time, but whenever they tried, I fell about laughing or someone came along and caught us.

Sometimes I went in to school, got my mark, then disappeared until lunchtime, when I went round the dinner room twice, got two dinners and was off again. Other times, my friends would answer the register for me. I paid off my friends to do my exams. I had pocket money, and little legacies came in from elderly relatives on my Dad's side (many ran pubs in the East End of London). Faking exams was easy. Our classroom had long bench-like desks, each of which accommodated eight pupils. Exam papers were laid out in advance and we all filed in and sat wherever we wanted. It was easy to create the illusion I was there. When the teacher called my name, a friend said, 'Here, sir', completed the paper and left it on the desk for collection. They were more trusting then.

One day, when I should have been at school, there was a knock on the door. I was playing rock and roll records, drinking my mother's port and just hanging out at home. On the doorstep was a Truant Officer. I told him I wasn't well. He didn't say anything to that, but his visit shocked me and I started to go to school more frequently for a while. Then I changed tactics and began forging notes to explain my absences. I'm very artistic. I can copy signatures.

To add a bit of excitement to my life and be different, I bought a sheath knife and started wearing it on my belt. When I was at school, I used to throw it at the toilet doors, never at people. I put thousands of holes in those doors, then someone told on me and I was expelled. That didn't worry me as I hated it anyway, and I could hang out round the café and eat pie, chips and beans with the local bikers. An older friend made arrangements for me to go to the local state school, and I was able to explain the change by telling my parents I'd been transferred. I was delighted when I discovered this school had a trip to France coming up in the spring of 1965. Now, I wouldn't have to spend my thirteenth birthday in Swindon. This was going to be my chance to bugger off on an adventure.

I wanted to go to Poland to lurk in the aura of the Countess Krystina, who had been my mother's best friend. Mum had told me stories about her; how she'd been stabbed to death by her jealous lover, Dennis Muldowney. The Countess was supposed to have worked for British Intelligence in World War Two. Mum met her after the war; she told me she liked to get away from the family sometimes and went down Soho to the jazz clubs. In one of the bars she got talking to the Countess who by then had taken the English name of Christine. They became close friends.

From the time I was very small I'd heard these stories, and Mum had sung me Polish lullabies; she said I was the reincarnated Countess because I was born around the time she was murdered. Against the family wishes, she took me down to Pentonville to gloat the day the murderer was hanged. She stared from across the road and cursed him with me in her arms. I was a few months old and this was my first experience of hatred. I became so involved with the story, I thought I was the Countess and used to draw pictures of myself in beautiful robes wearing a crown. It was all so ingrained on my mind that the need to get revenge for what Dennis did to Krystina has stayed with me and influenced certain actions I have taken in my life.

For the present, I prepared my plans by forging a letter from my friend Juliet's mother which said I'd be sleeping over there indefinitely after the school trip returned. My parents were tied up in their own problems. My mother had just had a still-born baby. She was devastated and near to a nervous breakdown. My staying at Juliet's house was a welcome break for them.

As the weekend for the trip approached, I packed my things in one of those big straw baskets which were fashionable then: underwear, spare skirt, sweater, make-up and my peg doll. She went everywhere with me. I'd made her a little Hell's Angel's outfit. I was mad about the Hell's Angels. Their leather-studded gear and the way they acted represented rebellion. That excited me.

I nicked some records from my Mum: 'The Flight of the Bumblebee', a couple of Elvis Presley's, a Julie London, Bill Haley's 'Rock around the Clock', 'Dance with a Dolly' and Paul Anka's 'Don't Gamble with Love'. I had £50 in cash saved from my pocket money, part-time jobs and from what Great Aunt Winifred left me. I wore my favourite outfit, a black polo-neck sweater and orange mini-skirt topped with my pride and joy: a black, fake fur bonnet which I saw as my first touch of glamour. I used it that weekend to cover my bouffant hairdo, as I needed to look older. What I was after now was a grown-up adventure.

When the coach came round the corner to collect me, I bent down to give our cat her last cuddle. Then, I was off with the kids. We took the A4 to London, cutting through the Earl's Court area on our way. This was where the Countess Krystina had lived and died. It made my urge to get to Poland even stronger. I went into action as soon as our ferry docked at Calais.

'I've got relatives in France,' I told our teacher, 'and I'm hoping to visit my Uncle Tom while I'm here.'

It sounds like a thin explanation now, but in those days, more than twenty-five years ago, it was all so much safer. Life was slower paced. People were more honest, so if you said something like that to your teacher, he would believe you and write it on his register. If there had been any doubt, I'd have done something more, like get a friend to phone later and say she was my Mum. I could see I'd got away with this from how he answered.

On the way to our hotel, we toured loads of war graves; then, after about an hour's driving, our coach pulled up outside a cheap, scruffy guest-house. We were divided into boys and girls on separate floors, so there was no chance of messing around like we'd been doing on the back seats of the bus.

Our first stop next morning was the Charles Heidsieck champagne cellars in Reims. When we arrived, all my friends posed for photographs beside street signs, but I chose a five-foot-high champagne bottle at the entry to the wine cellars. That champagne represented all the opulence and splendour – the lure of bright lights – that I wanted.

2

The Search for Excitement

Listening to the history of Charles Heidsieck was not my idea of fun. As the school party went round one corner of the wine cellars, I ducked away in the opposite direction. There were a few doors along the passage. I love lurking and I was nosey. I could hear some sort of movement in one of them as I went past, then suddenly this man came out and I thought, ooh, he's nice.

My favourite heroes at that time were swash-buckling cavaliers and highwaymen. He had that same look, a two-day stubble, shaggy black hair and he wore a red leather jacket. Even more fascinating, he was polishing a gun.

'*Bonjour, mam'selle.*' He invited me in for a drink. I was intrigued. I knew it was naughty and that I should be with the school group; that added to the moment. I could see he wasn't Mr Goody-Goody by the gun, and that appealed to me. If he'd stood there in a bowler hat holding a briefcase, I wouldn't have wanted to talk to him.

The room was small, crammed with racks of champagne covered in dust and cobwebs. On the floor, there were bottles of beer and bits of clothing, jeans and jumpers. The table was a door balanced on an empty crate, cards scattered over it where he'd been playing solitaire – no lights, only a flickering paraffin lamp. The furtive atmosphere excited me all the more. I had my schoolgirl French and he had some English; he said he was waiting for his friend who worked in the cellars.

'This is my twenty-first birthday present from my brother.' He showed off his gun, and handed it to me.

'I've never held a real gun before, isn't it heavy?'

'Be careful, it's loaded.'

I felt like a film star with it. First the champagne, now this. 'Why have you got a gun?'

'See everything, hear everything, say nothing.' He took it back. 'You'd better return to your teachers, *mam'selle*.'

We could hear the noise of my school group laughing and giggling. I felt he was only telling me this because he thought he should. I knew he fancied me so I had no intention of leaving if he'd let me stay. I stood up, brushing my lower parts close to him as I went past, and felt him get an erection against my legs.

'*Ma chérie*, you will have me arrested by the gendarmes.' What he said didn't seem to worry him, because he handed me an opened bottle of champagne. I settled down on one of the sweaters on the floor.

He began to tell me about himself. His name was Jacques but I called him Jake from then on. He told me his grandmother was a whore to the last king of Tahiti, which was why his friends called him 'The Prince'. I told him about my link with the Countess and how my parents had said I had delusions of grandeur. We clicked, it was like we were meant for each other. He wouldn't tell me why he had that gun but we sat chattering on, our languages all mixed up. I liked the way he spoke, it was really sexy with that French accent. Half the time, I didn't understand what he was saying. I suspect the same was true for him.

We began to kiss and cuddle. I was flirting with him, being deliberately provocative. He began teasing me with a wad of francs, rubbing them over my tits saying, 'Here's some money.'

I suppose, with his grandmother being a whore, he expected to pay for it.

'I'm a virgin, that's got to be worth more,' I said, all cheeky, even though I wanted him. I was more than ready, I had been wanting to do 'it' for ages. I'd spoken to my school friends who had and knew it was going to hurt. One of them said if you want it and you like the person, it's a delicious pain. I always remembered that. She also said, you mustn't fight, you have to go with it.

He put his jacket on the floor for me and I thought, oh, how gentlemanly, what a loving touch. He used a condom, which frightened me because I thought that the rubber would stick to my skin. I was aware of the pain, it felt to me like I was being poked in a place where there was really nowhere to be poked, but at the same time, because I liked Jake and wanted to do 'it', the fact it was painful made me feel all grown up. From my research with my school friends, I'd learned that the second time it wasn't so bad and the third time was even better till it didn't hurt at all. So, I was wanting to do it as many times as I could – and we did!

I heard the teacher call out and took no notice, assuming one of my friends would cover for me as usual. I don't know to this day if that's what they did, as too much has happened since then, but at that time Jake and I were in our own little world. After a while, he decided he wouldn't bother to wait for his friend, and asked me to come home with him for more sex in a more comfortable place.

His home took me by surprise. From the way he was dressed, I wasn't expecting such an impressive block of flats. It was all very opulent: fancy rosewood furniture trimmed with gilt, onyx and marble, tapestries on the walls and crystal chandeliers. It certainly wasn't cheap and tacky, it screamed money, and I felt an instant belonging to this lifestyle.

We both had baths, then we did all the stuff we didn't do in the cellar on a big, four-poster bed with an ice-blue, satin spread. On the cellar floor, it had been straight fucking, now he was showing me the A to Z of sex. After all that, we were both totally exhausted. I mean, I'd learned things I'd never known existed. We were probably in that bedroom for three hours. It was all loving and nice but I began to think, what am I going to do now? He could tell me to get out – was I going back to the school's hotel?

All sorts of thoughts were going through my mind. What had I done? Was I in trouble? Should I go on to Poland? As far as I was concerned, that idea was cancelled out. I was mad about Jake, I wanted to stay. The Prince had pushed the Countess into second place. I asked him if he wanted me to stay or should I go?

'Don't worry, *ma chérie*, I'll look after you.'

My fate was settled. I forged my last note to the school: 'I trust you will release my daughter to the care of her Uncle Tom. She will be spending some time with relatives in France.'

Jake went to the hotel, told the teacher he was my cousin, and they gave him my bag. People weren't suspicious in those days and I'd already mentioned that I was going to stay with my French relatives. It was that simple. After all, Swindon was not a sophisticated place. These people were honest and didn't act deviously, so they took you at your word. My teacher had no reason to disbelieve the note.

When Jake came back with my bag he wanted to chuck all my stuff in the garbage. He didn't like my clothes. (They were mostly synthetic so they wouldn't crease. I hate ironing.) We argued, and I ended up keeping my peg doll and my records. The rest went, and we were off shopping. Neither did he like the stuff I picked out. He said I had bad taste and taught me how to dress with style. I ended up with a selection of elegant, smart clothes, very twin-set-and-pearls, which made me look older.

I met his family. He didn't tell his Dad how young I was, as he would have disapproved. He thought I was seventeen. I looked much older than thirteen with my bouffant hair and the thick, dark eye make-up which was all the fashion then. Jake's father had a girlfriend. There was no mother, and it seemed a sore point so I never pursued it. They all took me to their hearts, and I finally felt I belonged. I was part of a family at last. Only later did I discover that they were all involved in organised crime. His brother wore hand-made suits and mohair coats. Jake was more casual and scruffy like his Dad, though when they were out on business they all looked very smart and blended in with the crowd.

Within a short time, I had created a completely new identity for myself. The French I'd learned at school was a godsend as I took on my new role as Jake's devoted 'wife'. I settled down and kept house for him. His favourite meal was T-bone steak, sauté potatoes, cabbage, mushrooms and corn. He was also partial to blue-vein cheese which I detested handling. His comings and goings brought in thousands of francs each week. My instincts told me not to ask questions and I followed his strict code. 'See everything, hear everything, say nothing.' That is something I still practise.

Sometimes I helped his father by delivering small brown paper parcels to various destinations. I'd wait on bridges, outside particular shops, street corners, car parks and landmarks, often disguised as a boy. A woman would come up to me, we'd exchange a password and I went on my way. It was always a different woman. Each time, I was paid 500 francs (about £50) with the odd present of a piece of jewellery. I suspected I was a courier for stolen gems, but it was safer not to know. I only did it because it was asked of me, and I felt obliged to run errands for this family that had taken me in. I wasn't frightened, this was part of my keep. By the time I'd reached fourteen, I was the owner of four diamond necklaces, seven diamond rings and a string of South Sea pearls. They were like trinkets to me; I'd already had the thrill of wearing jewellery when I used to nick my mother's diamond rings to wear to school.

All this time, I'd been phoning home every two weeks to tell my parents I was all right. They thought I was calling from my friend Juliet's house. They never questioned me and they never rang her. They believed I was being well looked after, and were used to all of us kids being out all the time. We were all loners anyway, all doing our own thing, even Mum and Dad who very rarely went out in each other's company. They had their problems and I, at least, was out of their hair.

When Jake's family got together, I was trusted because I was the 'wife'. Entertaining at home was exciting. I'd pour the drinks and listen. It was like watching a film. I liked that, it was an adventure just being around that crowd. If we were celebrating something, we ate together. At Jake's father's flat, his girlfriend did the cooking. It wasn't all that different to what I made, and I liked the fact we were a family together. Only once in a while, if it was some very special job, did they make me leave the room.

Towards the end of 1966, Jake decided we were moving to Paris. I didn't question anything he did. I liked our way of life. We lived well, travelled extensively visiting *châteaux* in France and sightseeing in other countries. I'd even been ski-ing in Switzerland. While we were there, Jake opened a joint bank account for us and a separate one in my own name. We were never short of anything, there was always champagne and wine in the fridge and plenty of food. I always cooked big portions for meals, like a banquet, then later ate the leftovers. I wasn't fat then, all that sex kept me active and slim!

In Paris, we had a huge, four-bedroom penthouse and new identities; Madeleine and Philippe du Bon. I chose the name Madeleine. The change came easy, as my Dad used to make up names when I was little. I remember when he took films to the chemist, he always left a false name. He never gave me any explanation for this so I ended up thinking it was not unusual to give phoney names and started doing it. Jake pretended he was the son of a wealthy industrialist from Lyons.

My days were spent doing nothing, just sleeping for hours. I'd always slept a lot, even when I was truanting from school. I'd read magazines, look round the shops, watch TV. There was a phase when I'd buy *Vogue* and similar magazines, and copy the make-up.

I'd sit for hours in front of a mirror messing around with make-up and hairstyles. Then, I'd shop and prepare dinner. When I didn't know the words for what I wanted to buy, I'd point. My cooking theory from school was very useful and being a person who liked to eat, it all came easily.

It wasn't long before gossip about this new 'millionaire' reached the ears of a famous Madame. There were dozens in France at that time. An invitation arrived for Jake to attend her New Year's Ball at the brothel. I was stunned by the invitation. In Swindon, there had been a café near the station where it was rumoured that prostitutes sometimes went. I'd hang around there, but never saw anyone I thought looked like one. I knew they got paid for having sex and used to think, ooooh, that's good getting paid. I didn't know anything else about it and asked Jake if I could go with him.

'Sure, *ma chérie*, you'll outshine all the whores put together.'

I dressed for the occasion in a stunning white rhinestone-studded evening gown which was part of a Paris fashion-house heist. We didn't go shopping any more, everything came in this way. The hardest thing was to decide which fur wrap to wear: the white mink or silver fox! I spent ages scraping my hair up into Jake's favourite Grecian goddess style. He wore a tuxedo. Our driver took us there with just half an hour to spare before midnight.

The Madame's house was a massive, double-fronted mansion. My first impression was of all the windows and the big front door. Inside, a black and white marble floor led to a ballroom from which a huge, carved oak staircase invited those in need up to fifteen bedrooms. There were fluted white columns, enormous gilt-framed mirrors on the walls, and a five-piece band in white tie and tails playing on a corner rostrum. Beautiful and elegant women reclined on purple velvet sofas. Others were draped around gentlemen's necks. To me, they all looked so mature and sophisticated but, I realised later, some were only sixteen.

Madame was a big, buxom Mama, elegantly but simply dressed, with one large piece of jewellery pinned to her gown.

'My, what a beautiful wife you have,' she told Jake, and then, in jest, pretended to offer me a job. 'I could make you rich, my dear.'

Jake was quite flattered that this woman thought so highly of me and turned to grin.

'Well, *ma chérie*, ask no questions, tell no lies.'

This was his way of saying business was business. He knew I belonged to him but he said later, if I wanted to tease some randy old goat for a 1,000 francs a time, then it was okay with him. Work was work, and you kept that separate from your private life.

Champagne flowed and as midnight approached, the guests gathered to count off the seconds. Madame stood in front of the band, raised her crystal goblet of champagne and toasted the wealth, health and happiness of all her dear customers. The New Year came in with everyone kissing and bras being ripped off by the women; the men were tossing around their shoes and wallets full of credit cards which amazed me, as did seeing those expensive crystal glasses smashed against the wall. It was a raucous party. I'd never seen anything like it. A couple of men pinched my bum and that pissed me off because I wasn't a whore and I felt, how dare they touch me.

Madame invited Jake to take his pleasure with any of her girls. He was, after all, the only one there with a 'wife'. All the other women present were whores.

'*Ma chérie*,' he asked, 'would you mind if I screwed every woman here?'

I couldn't refuse him anything, he was my Mr Wonderful. 'Go ahead, darling, Happy New Year.'

I passed the time with some of the other guests, astounded to discover that they included British diplomats and other rich and influential men. Madame's reputation for discretion had built her up an international collection of customers. I chatted to Sir Richard, a good-looking man who was British, and Ernst, an aged Russian aristocrat, who kept pinching my nipples.

'I'm not one of Madame's girls,' I snapped.

'Pity,' he said, 'I'd give anything for you to be mine for tonight.'

I wasn't interested. I thought I had everything I needed, but he persisted.

'I'll give you shares in my mine in Australia.'

'I'll think about it.' I fluttered my eyelashes. It did sound tempting.

Sir Richard asked me to dance; it was a slow, romantic number. He began rambling on about being the Governor of a Caribbean island with corrupt government officials which left me completely out of my depth. (This man was later to be assassinated.)

At 5 am, Jake emerged from his marathon. It hadn't tired his insatiable appetite and he still wanted me, so I wasn't jealous. It was me he was going home with. We said our goodbyes. As Madame kissed me farewell, she repeated her offer of employment. I ignored it.

Jake began to be more heavily involved in underworld activities and this frightened me. He was also away for longer periods. I found life without him very empty, and I didn't like being on my own. It was like being stuck in Swindon. I needed to find something else to do and I even thought about going home. If I did that, though, I might never get back to France and Jake. I was still a juvenile, and I could be picked up by the police in England. On balance, it was better to take my chances in Paris, so I went to look for Madame's card.

She was delighted to hear from me and said she'd send her chauffeur at once. I didn't know what to expect when I got there, but was game. When I was at the New Year's Eve party, I'd stored all the information about what was going on inside my brain. I'd been impressed by the friendly, loving atmosphere, like a family. The girls didn't seem as business-like as they do now. None had shown any resentment towards me.

When I arrived, Madame hugged me so tight she almost crushed my rib-cage. She drew me into her private office and told me the rules of the house.

I was fourteen going on nineteen.

'It's a 50–50 split. You keep all the presents. No arguments – always make the man feel like he's the best lover you ever had. And remember that the customer is always right, even when he's wrong.'

She gave me a contract to sign and poured two glasses of Bollinger. It should have been Charles Heidsieck since that's where this adventure had started.

'Welcome to the world of sin,' she said with raised glass. 'May it serve you as well as it has served me.'

We agreed that I would go into the salon and relax with a few more drinks, talk to the girls and then let her know when I felt ready to start. Loads of people remembered me from New Year's Eve. I was to be her 'English Rose'. Among the other girls were a couple of Americans and Australian; the rest were French. I was the youngest, while the others were between sixteen and thirty-five. We chatted for about an hour – small-talk about hair or clothes, we never talked shop. I found it easier to learn by watching. Men who approached and tried to join us were told to go to Madame and say who they would like. As soon as I felt comfortable with the situation, I gave Madame a nod and she brought over my first client – Bruno, a German musician. We went upstairs right away.

The bedrooms were all en suite, with TV, record player and a fancy bathroom stacked with men's toiletries. Madame had told me if I wanted to wash my clients I could, but most of them were already bathed, clean and groomed. A lot of them used to wear that clear nail varnish. Later, I learned that some did have a shower afterwards, particularly if they were going home to their wives.

Madame sent up champagne and Bruno bored me senseless with tales of Mozart and Brahms. I had to pretend to be interested but I didn't know what he was talking about. But because I was enjoying playing a new game, I made it seem that I knew about music. We did a lot of kissing and cuddling with the drinks. I was a bit pissed and took my dress down. Then, I wiggled around trying to do a striptease, which was a tip I had picked up from the other girls. Under my dress, I was wearing a purple waspie with black ribbons from Madame's dressing-up room. She had a selection of things we could wear to make us look horny.

I put on a fake French accent which made me feel sexy. Later, I did try to learn a bit more French but in the brothel I simply said '*oooh la la*' a lot. The other girls made that my nickname. They took the place of my estranged sister, and I loved having nearly twenty sisters I could admire and turn to. Madame had picked her girls for personality, loyalty and honesty. Any argumentative, unpleasant or bitchy girls were rejected, which was why we all got on so well.

Bruno went on talking about Beethoven. I wasn't to rush him, but I did encourage him to take off his shirt and ended up doing the undressing because he was so nervous! I found that men were more nervous of me because of my youth. In the bed, he was shy and I had to do all the leading which felt a bit strange because he was my first punter. I knew what to do anyway because of Jake, and I loved sex. We just had a straightforward screw, no variations. It was disappointing because his penis was only 2 inches long. I had to fake an orgasm and felt guilty taking his 1,000 francs. He asked for an appointment for the following week and on returning downstairs, I whispered to Madame, 'Next time I have him, please lend me your magnifying glass!'

I wasn't satisfied and thought, I'll have to find another customer.

Old Ernst was hovering in the background. I would call his bluff about that mine. I led him upstairs to the Pink Room with the round bed. Ernst seemed ancient, his skin all white and crinkled like crepe paper, but I remembered Madame's advice: 'Good whores detach all personal emotions', and was his for the night. What he lacked in looks was compensated by his 9 inch penis. That didn't have a wrinkle on it.

I gave him a taste of my special breast smothering. Even at that age, my boobs were 40 inches compared to my 20 inch waist. (They'd always been bigger than everyone else's: at eleven, I got my first bra, size 34B, which was white with little pink flowers. Probably in jealousy, the other girls said my tits were puppy fat.) For Ernst and other punters, I used to make up a story about how I'd smothered all my six husbands by turning over on top of them in the night and there was nothing the police could do about it. They loved it when I used to say: 'I'm going to smother you in my tits and take all your money.'

We had lots of fun. Ernest had some very kinky ideas which included me riding round the room on his back, slapping his bare bum and using my black stockings as reins. He didn't give me any shares that night, but four weeks later, after I'd become his regular three times a week, the mine and mineral rights were my bonus. He was very rich, but then all the other clients were rich too. Even the 'poor' ones were rich: impoverished aristocrats with estates and treasures, although no cash in their pockets.

I loved it there. The money came in and also beautiful pieces of jewellery as presents – necklaces, earrings and bracelets. I enjoyed wearing the lovely clothes too, and they didn't get much wear and tear. My greatest expenditure was on stockings, which got snagged and laddered a lot, mostly by the clients' whiskers!

On Sundays, Madame took us all to church. She insisted: 'Although we are sinners, if we go to church and are kind to children and animals, we will go to heaven.' Church was a new experience for me. I didn't understand the hymns but somehow, in another language, they were special.

Madame ran the brothel with great style. There were two entrances, the impressive one at the front which led to beautifully gowned women, and a more modest one at the back. There, men queued for a cheaper service, and sometimes got more than they realised. When business was slow in the salon, the girls changed clothes and accommodated the lower end of the market!

Madame taught us etiquette and grooming, and for an hour every day she made us exercise our vaginal muscles! We had to clench them tightly and release them a thousand times, so she could keep passing us off as 'virgins'.

While I was working there, Jake was a man of his word and never questioned me, but his trips away were getting longer and longer. I felt he had deserted me. In a huff, I wrote him a note saying I was going home to think things over. I'd gone off the idea of Poland by now and fancied returning to England. I wanted to see if Jake would miss me.

I was confident that I wasn't on the missing juvenile list because I'd kept in touch with my parents regularly. They were still accepting my story that I was living with Juliet, and that I had a little part-time job (with a grocery van that went round the estates). They hadn't seen much of me when I lived at home anyway, so it didn't make a lot of difference to them that I wasn't there.

I didn't plan to go back and live at home. I had plenty of money. I always made sure I had money, and that was something else I'd learned from my father who had money tucked away in various accounts and building societies. Through Jake's family connections, I had a choice of four passports and other documents if I needed them. I felt I was safe to return to England, ready to let the wind blow me in any direction it chose.

3

Rags and Riches

I came back ready for a new scene – something totally different. I'd relished my role as a whore in a Parisian brothel, but was now quite happy to try something else. This willingness to adapt was to be the key to my life. I came back with a sense of independence: I was going to take care of myself. London offered the chance of a new adventure, and if I could get in with the Hell's Angels crowd so much the better. I'd been mad about them since I was a kid, and was crazy about motor bikes (even now, I can't pass one without stopping to look it over). I knew where the Hell's Angels hung out in London, as one of my friends at school had an older brother who zoomed around in leathers. Some of the time I'd been truanting from school I'd been round and had a look at the places where they hung out. I knew where to go.

First, I had to dress the part. I bought a new pair of leather jeans, denim jacket, black polo-neck sweater, and black leather platform-soled boots in Oxford Street. Those boots were also going to be my bank; I'd be able to stash my money down them. I changed into my new self at Paddington Station and left the rest of my things in a locker.

Now, I was ready to lurk around the bikers' haunts. The main place then was the Macabre Coffee Bar in Meard Street in Soho. It was a marvellous place with tables made from wooden coffins and seats like tombstones. I sat on John Brown's 'grave' tucking into steak and kidney pie, chips and beans. This was my first English meal for ages, and it went down a treat. After that, I hitch-hiked round some of the other places where bikers gathered, like the pie stalls at Whipps Cross, Forest Gate, Chelsea Bridge and the Ace Café on the North Circular Road.

Dressed as I was, I became part of the crowd. Everyone was friendly; I was flirty with the guys who took me off on high-speed runs down the North Circular. It was as if Paris never was, except for the fact in France I'd got by with my bit of French and here I had enough bikers' slang to fit in with no trouble. There were plenty of places where I could crash out, and a crowd of us once dossed down on the rubbish tip opposite the Ace Café. There was always the odd bit of carpet to keep you warm. Whatever I might be reduced to in the future, it certainly won't be worse than life on a rubbish dump!

Then I heard that Hell's Angels and Hippies were also bunking up at the deserted Arts Laboratory in Drury Lane. Once I had sorted out who was the leader of this gang, I made a play for him. Rat wasn't in Jake's league. He had a greenish, rolled gold earring in his left ear, and tattoos all over his arms. Some were rude words. I didn't fancy him sexually but what he did have that appealed was the privilege of his own room in the loft. Everyone else was crashing out on the dirty floor under the stage. I was able to keep his attempts at lovemaking at bay with promises that we could start once my 'heavy' period had finished.

Because I have always been able to step in and out of parts, I fell easily into the way this crowd were living. I should have been an actress! It appealed to me because it was so different to the life I'd left behind in France and I wasn't bored any more.

When it came to food, the group divided up; some used to go off for hamburgers and chips, but I found it more fun to join the vegetarians. We used to trail round Covent Garden after the traders had packed up for the day. They nearly always left enough for us to collect the makings of an evening stew which we cooked in a big dented pot over a fire made of wood pinched from the building renovations all around us. Those were the days when the area was still a bit of a dump, not all bright and shiny like it is now.

We moved en masse when we found a huge, empty building in Broad Court. It had loads of rooms, a lovely big staircase and a courtyard in the middle which I used to love to walk round. This place was directly opposite the Bow Street police station. We weren't bothered, we weren't breaking the law, just squatting. Once the word got out that there was a bit of privacy in this place, we had a congregation of lesbians, prostitutes, down-and-outs and junkies to add to the Hell's Angels. We became one big rowdy family.

This scenario quickly came to end when my head started to itch. Rat's bit of beard and eyebrows were itchy too. Everyone said he had caught crabs from 'Quick Fix Lil', the junkie slag who was in the end room of the second floor. Suddenly it wasn't so much fun. I went to find a doctor who told me I had head lice from sleeping on dirty bedding. That, added to the fact that Rat was becoming aggravated waiting for my 'period' to finish, indicated it was time to go.

My attempt to sneak away in the night failed when I disturbed a character called 'Toothless Victor'. By telling him I knew a man who had some grass, he followed quietly. I managed to lose him in the maze of streets around Covent Garden. What I needed most was a bit of privacy to deal with my head lice. Dressed as I was, all scruffy, that limited where I could go. I sat on the Circle Line trying to decide what to do for the best. After I'd made several round trips, one of the women porters asked me where I was going. I pretended I'd fallen asleep and got off at the next stop, which was how I discovered that Gloucester Road tube station had the biggest and best toilet cubicles.

The stuff the doctor had given me had to stay on my hair for an hour. I sat out the time in one of the loos reading a comic I'd found. The liquid hand soap then made a very nice shampoo, and by ducking down, the hand dryer became just as useful. There was a large toilet, big enough for me to stretch out, and so I took a nap which lasted until the cleaning lady came in next morning.

The next stop on the tube was Earl's Court. It drew me like a magnet: those stories of the Countess and her murder were always at the back of my mind.

A permanent feature of the Earl's Court Road was the pie stall. The proprietors were friendly and invited me to have my tea and hot dog inside where it was warm. When they began to ask questions, I suspected they knew I was under-age and might report me to the police. I became evasive and knew I needed to get away. Outside, lorry drivers were arriving for breakfast – just parking in the road. It was quite legal then, which is funny when you think how busy that area is now. Flirting and prick-teasing with men came easy to me so I soon had an offer of a ride which included a 'service' for £2. I didn't need the money, I had a hefty wad stashed in my boot. Here was a chance to get away and the driver was a different kind of man to any I'd tried so far. He said his name was John, but I was to learn they were all called John!

I spent the next few months with lorry drivers, hitch-hiking up and down the country. My instincts told me it was better to stay on the move. I had an inviting, knowing smile which let the men know I was willing to be naughty. The going rate was between ten shillings (50p) and £3. They would offer. I used to barter, depending on my mood.

'Wanna earn a few bob?'

'Cost you a fiver.'

They'd say, 'I'll give you . . .'

I'd say yes or no.

In one day, I went from London to Derby four times. I palled up with a girl called 'Welsh' (she came from Wales) who said she knew a few gypsies working at the Goose Fair in Nottingham, and we could make a few pounds. Then she buggered off and left me on my own. I got a job on the 'Tip the Lady' sideshow wearing a black nylon nightie with fringes round the edges. When the punters hit a target, the seat tilted and I was tipped on to the floor. My poor legs were soon black and blue. It was just as well I was quick to pick up the gypsy slang, because after a few days I was warned that the men were saying if I didn't 'open my meat', I'd be in trouble. Apparently all thirty-seven were planning to gang-rape me. I escaped and went back on the road.

The transport cafés on the motorways and trunk roads became my home. I knew the proprietors, the regular truckers and the regular girls. We were all in a similar situation. One plump and pathetic girl came into one of the cafés, sporting a nasty black eye, and I felt sorry for her. Later, she returned the compliment by loaning me a sweater when it was cold. She'd said, 'Come to my wardrobe and get it.' I followed her to a clump of bushes about a quarter of a mile away where she had her clothes hidden in a carrier bag. I was really surprised. She would keep it there under the bushes for weeks at a time, coming back to change every so often! Doreen and I became the best of friends, and were to remain so for years.

We girls used to play the pinball machines while we were talking to the men. Once, a proprietor's wife caught me flirting and talking dirty to her husband. She beat me up and threw me out of the café.

My basket of belongings came after me and everything spilled into the mud. I felt so humiliated and didn't go back to that café again.

I was never on the breadline at this time. I could always dig money out of my boot for a bed-sit, so I could refuse any punter I didn't fancy. But because I was thrifty with my money, I figured out places where I could sleep in the daytime. You'd be amazed how easy it is to take a nap while sitting in a church pew pretending to pray. Another good wheeze was to go to a library, find the biggest encyclopedia on the shelves, prop it on a table and sleep behind it. Keeping clean wasn't difficult either: you could have a good wash in the public toilets or swimming baths. It was a shilling for a bath and 1/6d (7½p) with a towel. All this may have seemed a far cry from life in Paris, but that in a way was what made it appealing. I wasn't sitting around waiting for something to happen any more.

I hung out a lot at the service stations on the M1. Sometimes the men bought me food – egg, bacon, sausage, chips and beans. They always asked for a mug of tea at 'transport prices'. It was at one of these that I got involved in the High Life again, this time with a British Duke. I was first approached by his chauffeur who offered me five crispy £20 notes to follow him to a Rolls Royce with white leather seats. I was duly delivered to the gatehouse of a country estate and told to wait. The place was creepy, and looked as if it was the dump for all the unwanted stuff from the main house. I remember an ugly, stuffed carp staring at me through its glass case; cracked blue and white china plates hung on the walls.

A middle-aged man came in wearing an old jumper and trousers. 'How old are you, my dear?'

'Nineteen.'

'How old?' His posh voice was sarcastic.

'Well, er, fifteen – umm, fourteen really, but I'll be fifteen soon.'

'Splendid.' He led me up a wooden staircase to a bedroom done in faded pink and green chintz. 'Take off your clothes and stand on your head.'

'What?'

'Don't be difficult, darling, I like it that way.'

Always obedient, I stripped off and balanced upside down, my head resting on the pillow, my bum against the headboard and my legs up on the wall.

His Grace approached. Upside down, I was now eye level, or

rather mouth level for him to give me oral sex. I was to find out he always liked to be comfortable.

'Thank you, Your Grace.' What a weird set-up!

On the way back down to the motorway service area, the driver told me I was a lucky girl, as the Duke wanted me on a regular basis. Then, he pulled the Rolls into a lay-by and clambered into the back seat, £50 in hand.

'My turn now.'

Arrangements were made for me to be picked up every Wednesday at 2 pm. I managed that easily by hitch-hiking. To cover my contortions, my price went to £200 and was accepted. I nicknamed the Duke 'Pellet', because he had a tapered cock. After our third meeting, we had full sex.

'I like to get to know a girl first,' he explained.

Because he paid so well, when he insisted on sex without a condom I felt obliged to take a chance. But it wasn't only sex with him. We spent time together, and talked about current events. I was learning all the time. I had and still have an insatiable appetite for information of all kinds. He used to tell me tales of the aristocracy and hereditary titles. He actually invited me to a Hunt Ball. I had an appropriate dress, a black lace and chiffon cocktail number I'd bought at Selfridges. While my travelling gear was jeans, polo-neck sweaters and jacket, I always kept something good in my bag – just in case. With black stiletto sling-back shoes, I was able to mingle with the guests.

The ball was another new experience. I lurked around basking in the ambiance and danced with a few men. 'Pellet' kept a watchful eye on me. He had told me before to behave myself and be discreet. If spoken to I was to reply as briefly as possible, then make an excuse and retreat to the restroom. I wasn't impressed with the food, and thought some of the upper-crust guests were pompous gits! One girl bragged to me that a popular designer had made her red, puffed, taffeta gown. It was horrible, she looked like a giant tomato. No-one there suspected I was an under-age whore! I have no idea how the Duke explained who I was, possibly a friend of a friend. He must have got a buzz out of the fact I was there. From then on, we began to spend more and more time together. I didn't see any other man, the Duke became my sugar daddy.

Being with one man again made me compare this relationship with the one I'd had with Jake. My feelings for him were no different in spite of the fact he had neglected me. So in June 1967, I returned to Paris.

There was a café near the Gare du Nord where Jake was known, so I went there first. I needed to find out if he had found another girl. Once I knew he was on his own I phoned. He hadn't done very well while I was gone – there'd been too much drinking and gambling – and he was glad to see me. He knew I didn't like his work and, to be fair, agreed I could go back to the brothel. 'I have my job, you have yours. Ask no questions, tell no lies.'

His only concern was that I should not get diseased or pregnant. I was welcomed back by all the clients, including my regulars like Ernst and Sir Richard. Jake's jealousy grew with my popularity. He monitored my progress in order to 'look after me'. His father monitored me as well. This was normal with the family to make sure no-one was grassing up any secrets. I never did reveal any secrets and earned a respect in the underworld which I still enjoy today. In the end, to ensure I couldn't continue at the brothel, Jake deliberately began to shag me to death. I was too sore to work and had to agree to stay at home with him.

While Jake was playing poker one night soon after this, there was an ambush by a rival gang. The fight was over territory. This was hard-core, organised crime. Their motto was 'shoot first, ask questions later'. Several of his pals were killed and he was badly wounded. I didn't know this for some time. I sat and worried for three days but didn't do anything. I had been taught to keep calm and that if Jake ever went missing, not to raise the alarm but wait for advice from the family. Finally, his brother came to tell me that Jake was in hospital, but I couldn't see him because Interpol were watching all his visitors.

I needed a diversion from this worry and decided to go back to the brothel. It wasn't long before I began to realise I'd missed my periods. I was pregnant. I couldn't believe it at first. All the customers at the brothel wore condoms and I knew none of them had broken. My diary confirmed what I suspected. 'May 1967. "Pellet".' I was bearing the child of nobility.

There was no point in notifying His Grace. He was part of my past life. He would probably have given me money, but what good was that without his commitment and responsibility? I examined my options, which were very few. It was folly to try to keep a baby in my situation. I was under-age, the child would be taken from me and put in a home or institution. I sought the advice of Madame, and she told Ernst with whom, by now, I had become very close. He had no heir and immediately wanted to adopt the baby. That seemed the perfect solution. I owed it to my child to give him or her the best possible life.

Madame arranged for me to be moved to a smaller brothel which would be a more discreet hiding place. The whores there fussed round me like a load of aunts. They even knitted booties and jackets. To pay for my keep, with my limited French, I managed to take messages, opened letters and arranged them on Madame's desk, and did other odds and ends. Madame was like a mother – I felt safe and looked after.

Gossip about my predicament travelled through the underground to Jake in the hospital. I heard back that he was furious and insisting I should visit him. I was ready to take the chance. With the help of my friends at the brothel, I devised a crazy plan for which I needed the assistance of a priest. Luckily we had one who was a regular client!

Among the selection of costumes in the brothel – kept for our customers' requirements – was a nun's habit. This covered my swollen belly. Off the priest and I went to the hospital. I was frightened and excited at the same time, desperate to see Jake but worried about his reaction. When we arrived, to keep up the charade and stay in character, we had to visit every bed in the ward with a few comforting words. Finally, I reached Jake. I was horrified by all the tubes and bandages. I wanted to hug and kiss him, but didn't dare, as it wouldn't have looked right. I had to content myself with whispers so that he knew who I was.

His response was a sad smile. 'What are you doing with another man's child? Do you not love me any more?'

I felt awful. I lied and told him that a client's condom had burst – it's an occupational hazard. I promised I wouldn't keep the baby. I only cared about him and wanted him to recover. I told him we'd have a child of our own when he came out of the hospital. The more I told him how much I loved him, the happier he became. By the time I left, he had forgiven me.

In January 1968, preparations were made in the brothel for the baby's birth. To forestall any unexpected official difficulties, Madame had checked to make sure it would not be illegal for a child to be on the premises. She discovered that the age limit was three before the authorities would interfere. Ernst wanted to be there, and a client who was also a doctor offered his services. To be doubly sure that all went well, Madame also called in one of the top 'underground' midwives.

I gave birth to a healthy, seven-pound son, but to everyone's surprise I turned away and asked the would-be father, Ernst, to take over. All I could do was cry. I dared not look at the baby for fear I would become attached to him and unable to go through with the plan. I had to concentrate on the fact that I was in love with Jake, and this wasn't his baby. I had to believe that my little one stood a better chance in life without me.

Rapid arrangements were made for the adoption. Everyone was cagey about where the child would be raised. It was not to be in France. I was assured long-term plans would be made for my son's future education. When he was four weeks old, I revoked my rights to motherhood with Ernst's gold fountain pen. I agreed not to speak of this or contact my son until he was twenty-five, then he could make up his own mind about me. I have often wondered where he is and what he is doing. I was terribly upset about parting with the baby and Ernst was concerned for me. Madame told him to leave me alone to return to the life I knew best.

I was devastated. I was barely sixteen and felt like I was fifty. I returned to Jake's apartment. He was still in hospital but his brother came round every so often to make sure I was all right. I became obsessed with exercising to regain my figure, wanting Jake desperately so nothing else mattered. I pushed thoughts of my son out of my head. If I didn't think about it, it couldn't hurt me. I cleaned the flat. I boiled my jewellery in saucepans of water with household soap powder added to clean it. Jake's father told me this trick of the trade was better than any jewellery cleaner on the market.

One day I heard that Jake would be coming home that evening. I was there waiting to pounce on him at the door with kisses. Jake insisted I should put the baby out of my mind. 'We shall never speak of this again.'

For a few short months, life slipped into a routine and I was happy to stay at home and keep house for him. Then Jake began accepting contracts that were very dangerous. Every time there was a knock on the door, I trembled, wondering if someone was going to tell me he was dead. It was all too much for me. With the constant fear and tension, and postnatal depression, I was probably traumatised at that time. I realised I couldn't go on this way and decided to make another try at life in London.

I brought back enough money to keep me going; the rest of my money and my jewellery was stuffed in one of the hidey-holes Jake and I kept under the floorboards of the flat. If it disappeared, I didn't care. I had more than enough for a new set of leathers and a return to the Hell's Angels scene. I made straight for the Chelsea Bridge pie stall. There was still a need for me to keep on the move in England and that pie stall was the handiest place to pick up lorry drivers. I was officially a juvenile till I was twenty-one, and I was a long way from that.

I went back to a sleazy, bed-sit life, but for me at that time it didn't matter. One of the dumps I stayed in was particularly memorable because it was so awful. The rent was £2 a week for a room over a poultry shop off Petticoat Lane in East London. To wash, I had to use the sink in the hall which was horrible – covered in slime and mould. I later moved on to a better place in Chiswick.

I was doing all right as a 'lorry girl' until I met up with two ex-bikers at the pie stall at Thornton Heath Pond. They were driving a van down to Brighton. I would never usually take off with two men, but I'd seen them hanging around this place before. They seemed part of the gang – talking bikers' slang and such – so I thought I'd be safe with them. When we got to Pease Pottage, without any warning, one of them said, 'Take your knickers off.'

'I'd rather walk,' I protested.

There was no chance of that. I was in the back of the van and they weren't going to let me out. I had some money in my boot, but thought I'd better not resist or they would beat me up, rob me, then I'd have nothing. It was better to give in. I'll never forget Pease Pottage. Those men were disgusting – repulsive. One had green teeth, he was a slimey toerag, but I couldn't see the point of struggling. They were going to rape me regardless, so I just lay there. Boy, was I angry. It was the first time I'd had sex against my will.

What made it worse was that both of them had the cheek to do it twice. Then, they took me down to Brighton beach and had another go. It was in the early hours of the morning, so there were very few people around. Anyway, I didn't call for help because I couldn't risk having the police come along and discovering I was under-age. There was nothing I could do. I threw away my knickers and sat in the sea trying to wash away what they had done. I blamed myself for what had happened. I'd broken the golden rule about hitch-hiking: never hitch with two men.

I got back to London as soon as I could and immersed myself even more into the Hell's Angels scene by buying a second-hand BSA C15 bike. It cost me £15. Of course, as usual, I used a false name. I'd gone through a few by then: Madeleine du Bon, the bejewelled Paris whore; Goldie Moran, when I was a hitch-hiker in denim and chains; 'Lady Scratch' on the biker scene, the first because I've always identified with that regal, Countessy aura, and the second because I had long nails! (I thought it was glamorous to have long, painted finger nails.) I loved being outrageous, to switch names to go with the parts I was playing. In many ways, I see where I was still like a kid, always eager for adventure. And this in spite of all I'd been up to, which wasn't exactly a traditional childhood.

I hung out at the pie stall on Chelsea Bridge a lot and got friendly with a man called Norman. He offered me the share of his bed-sit in Lambeth. It was seedy and horrible. He used to keep a bucket of dirty socks and pants soaking and he picked his nose. I only stayed for a couple of days. For some stupid reason, though, I thought I could trust him, so I used to talk about my parents. He'd been hoping I'd sleep with him, and when I refused he betrayed my confidence and grassed on me.

The police came along to the pie stall and took me and my bike to Nine Elms police station. While I waited, I used a hairclip to dig my name in the woodwork. Naturally, it was 'Lady Scratch', my bike-scene name. I wonder if it's still there? The police had phoned my father, and suddenly he was there to collect me. He had to take the bike as well as me. Getting it to Paddington railway station and up into the goods van wasn't easy. Dad was not pleased. Not a word was said on the journey home.

He sent me to my room.

My sister was sarcastic, even after all those years. 'Oh back again, are you? Don't think you're going to nick my clothes.' Nothing had changed there.

By then, my brothers had left home and were in bed-sits, so I never saw them.

Mum came up later. My first impression was, hasn't she got thin. She must have lost three stone since losing that baby, and since I'd left. She was obviously not a well woman. She sat on the bed. 'What's all this in the diary?'

My father had been handed the diary with the rest of my belongings. It had been a Christmas present from an aunt – a five-year diary with lock and key.

'What diary?'

She asked me if it was true about the baby. I wouldn't answer. She asked me other questions like, had I been doing all those things in the diary and: 'Who's Jake?'

I stayed on the defensive. 'Jake who?'

We sat through an embarrassing silence. There was nothing I could say to her. She left the room. Sitting on the bed I looked out of the window and felt trapped. It took a week for my parents to decide what to do with me. I either stayed in my room and read magazines or listened to Radio Caroline, or saw a few old friends. We swopped sexual experiences but I don't think they'd done quite as much as I had!

In the end, my father thought it would teach me a lesson if I was put into a Home for Wayward Girls. No-one learns anything in such places except how to be worse. One girl showed me how to pick locks. As with all new arrivals, my money, watch, earrings and bracelets were confiscated by Matron. I was given a change of clothes, Oxfam style. It was very spartan and strict. There were mountains of potatoes to peel and long stone corridors to polish. The rest of the time we had a lounge where we could chat, draw or write letters. Parents could visit: my father came once; my mother was too ill to travel.

We were ten to a dormitory and I made friends with one girl who was of Far Eastern origin. She had lovely long black hair which I used to plait for her. We sang folk songs together at night. Another girl, who hated me, had laddered her tights. She stole mine from my bedside locker while I was asleep. I recognised them because of their particular pale shade. After that, I kept my tights under the mattress and slept on them.

After we had our wash in the evening, we had to scrub our underwear. I always remember that long row of white basins. We had to leave our knickers draped over them to dry. Someone swopped my clean knickers for hers. They were all stained and horrible. Matron didn't believe me when I complained and for punishment, I had to wash everyone else's knickers. It was a dreadful place and I hope it's been closed down.

Going out, we were treated like schoolchildren, two by two in a line. I began to consider escape. My photographic memory took in every detail of roads, walls and buildings. The second time out, I absconded by skipping over a church wall. A bus came along and I got on, but I didn't have any money, so I apologised and got off at the next stop. That didn't matter, I was free again!

4

On the Game

I walked along to a busy junction and found a suitable hitch-hiking spot. A trucker pulled up.

'Wanna lift, luv?'

It was music to my ears after the days of 'Do this! Do that!' He was heading east to London, to Billingsgate market with a load of fish, but I'd have gone anywhere just to get off the streets before the cops spotted me. His name was Taffy, a stocky, rugged man in his early forties, wearing a kind of Hell's Angels hat.

I was hungry and saw no point in beating around the bush. I told him I was on the game and working my passage to London. We negotiated a fee – £5 plus egg and chips at the transport café for 'full sex with a rubber'. He asked to do it first and eat later, because he couldn't 'ride' on a full stomach. I agreed (I was of the same opinion anyway). Taffy pulled up at a convenient lay-by – just past Chippenham on the A4 – took a crumpled 'packet of three' from the glove compartment and unzipped his flies. 'Money first,' I said. After all, Madame's 'pay later' rules didn't apply to passing trade on the road, especially men like him, with a dog-end hanging from the corner of his mouth and fag ash embedded in his matted hairy chest. I stuffed the fiver up the cuff of my blouse, took one leg out of my tights and knickers, and climbed on to his lap, straddling his erection.

Afterwards, he fed me at the Golden Arrow café near Marlbrough, then we continued to London, not stopping until he filled up with petrol at a 24-hour garage. I couldn't believe my luck. I was in Earl's Court, as if the Countess Krystina was drawing me back to her.

I got out to stretch my legs. 'Phew! You don't 'alf pen and ink!' remarked the garage manager. He was right. The pungent smell of Taffy's load was clinging to my clothes. As Taffy and I parted company, he gave me his hat. I could decorate it with chains and studs and wear it when next I hit the bikers' scene.

The garage manager introduced himself as 'Alf the night man' and let me wash in his toilets. He cottoned on that I was a young runaway, and enticed me into his night man's hut with cheese sandwiches and a flask of tea.

He took me downstairs to a basement restroom which was filled with tatty chair cushions, old tyres, an enamel sink and a gas cooker.

'You can kip down 'ere.'

'Thanks.'

'Wanna earn a few bob?'

'Yes!'

Dozens of taxi drivers frequented Alf's garage throughout the night, not just for petrol, but to talk shop. Between them they also ran a blue-film syndicate. I was surprised by his terminology: 'Jump in the old flowery [flower 'bed'] with the men I bring round and you'll get £3 a time.' I took him up on the offer and over the next few weeks, at nights, I hung around the garage and got back in funds. There was no shortage of men wanting to screw a willing young teenager, and they paid Alf a commission for the pleasure. More often than not, I managed to push their fee up to £5 by saying, 'Oooh, do you fancy doing it the Continental way?' Then we'd have sex in an unusual position and I'd talk dirty in French!

I built up a steady stream of regular clients consisting of Chinese waiters from a Fulham Road restaurant and all the cab drivers from the Pont Street shelter. (These green, wooden oblong huts are no longer used, they're just relics of London's past.) One night Alf pulled a fast one and invited a group of his pals around for group sex; they paid me £30 by cheque. When I went to deposit it in my newly opened post-office account in Chiswick, I discovered it was a 'dud', written on a shop-bought cheque book – not even drawn on a bank. I was so embarrassed. The teller looked at me as if I was mad and afterwards I walked the length of Chiswick High Road cursing myself for being so gullible. Jake and Madame had been my mentors, but neither had told me about fake cheques. When I confronted Alf with this, he made out he didn't know. I thought this was bad, because I was only young and he had taken advantage of me.

Alf then arranged for me to put on a strip show for ten cabbies at the Pont Street shelter, and I went there at 2 am one morning. It was cute and dinky inside, about 5 foot wide by 12 foot long with the entrance at one end, and a cooking range at the other. A greasy cook fried eggs, bacon and bread, serving it up with mugs of tea from a hissing silver urn. He put his egg slice down when I arrived and joined the audience sitting along two wooden benches either side of a long wooden table. This time I made them pay in advance, and they each chipped in ten bob which I collected in a soup bowl. I provocatively took off my blouse in time to the beat of the music on the radio. Next off came my bra, shoes, tights and knickers. I kept my skirt on in order to offer 'private' open-leg shots to men willing to insert silver coins into 'my moneybox'.

Near the garage was the Paris Pullman cinema. The projectionist was a petite young man in his twenties called Pete, who dabbled in nude photography and movies on super 8 cine-film. For a laugh I posed for a few snaps, but when he asked me to take my knickers off I charged him a fiver for explicit shots provided my face wasn't showing. (God forbid if my father ever saw them!)

Whilst bumming round in the daytime, I bumped into Doreen again at a roadside café. She was down on her luck so I took her along to meet Alf and Pete. She was very promiscuous, preferring to give it away rather than sell it, and together we performed in a blue film. She did it for free, I charged £15. The title was *Arty Snood's Talent Contest*. We danced around the cinema stage in leather mini-skirts with bath-plug chains draped around our breasts, singing 'Vibros are a girl's best friend' to the classic Marilyn Monroe tune. This was the late sixties, so it was pretty harmless compared to today's standards.

Pete screened his films at a private members' club in Fulham Road. A man called 'Clean Machine Dave' had converted his basement flat into a small cinema. There were six rows of red velvet seats and every Saturday the punters paid £2 to get in, a price which included sandwiches and tea. The doors opened at midnight and a mixture of feature films, cartoons and blue movies were shown until 6 am. I doubled as waitress/usherette and also made the sandwiches (half of which I ate). Games were played too, like who could guess the funniest name for men's genitals. The proverbial 'meat and two veg' was always put forward, but I won every time with names like 'gun and two bullets' and 'night flyer and two hangars'.

I had an even better chance to show off my talents when one of the cabbies introduced me to a friend who ran a string of Soho nightclubs. It was my 44DD tits that were auditioned. I joined his strippers and developed a suitably sleazy routine to Adam Faith's 'Beat Girl'. My props were a purple feather boa, a black lace Spanish fan, a pair of purple sequinned nipple tassels, and a matching G-string with long pink ribbons trailing down from the sides. From the early days at Madame's, I knew that my tits were my biggest asset, so I spent hours prancing about in front of a mirror until I learned to do something special with them. By accident I discovered that holding one arm up in the air and jumping up and down made my tits swing in opposite directions. I practised this until I could control different speeds. My act was unique and I became popular on the strip circuit.

In those days each club had about ten or twelve girls. Each girl was paid ten shillings for a three-minute 'spot', then she rushed to the next club, did that spot, then on to the following club and so on until the circuit was completed within thirty to forty minutes. Girls who were late missed their spots and lost the money. There is a phrase 'to go case' which means to sleep with someone on a 'one-off' basis. I learned that this saying derives from the days when strippers carried their props in little vanity cases from club to club, popped in, stayed a short time, and left.

From there I moved up the ladder to topless barmaiding in a hostess club (where men pay for a woman to sit with them). Men would push fivers into my deep cleavage as an excuse to fondle me, and this caused jealousy and animosity from staff less well endowed, so I left after a month. Nothing satisfied me for long. I was constantly searching for new adventures and absolutely revelled in the decadent ambiance of Soho.

I decided to go on the game full time, and whenever a likely punter walked past, my opening line was 'Business?' Interested ones replied 'How much?', disgusted ones scurried by, and those interested for an alternative reason said 'You're nicked'!

It was during this time that I met 'Mad Mustapha', a Maltese client whom I picked up in Piccadilly. He took me to his flat and paid me £10 to act out a weird scenario. I was game for anything, but with him the most difficult thing to do was keep a straight face! He gave me a number nine golf club and a ball with 'Chamber Pot Championship' written on it. Then he placed an old-fashioned china piss pot on the top tread of the staircase, and lay down at the opposite end of the hallway. First of all he masturbated until stiff, then he took a piece of black plasticine and moulded it around the end of his erection to form a little concave platform. My job was to place the golf ball on top of the plasticine platform, swing my club in readiness and shout 'Yes!' as I teed off. He never liked pain, but the danger of it turned him on. I could easily have missed the ball and whacked his penis, causing serious damage. But this was a risk he loved to take and it made him ejaculate. The ball rolled along the passage and plopped off the landing into the awaiting potty.

Sometimes Doreen hung out with me around Soho, eventually taking my advice and refraining from giving freebies. Her speciality was 'cut-price gobbles' to Pakistanis at ten bob each or three for a pound. She loved it, and she even 'swallowed' (something I have never done). She said semen was good for her because it contained vitamins and the sucking made her face muscles firm!

Sometimes I had to wait whilst she got through twenty waiters from the Indian restaurants so I'd amuse myself by watching Bugs Bunny in the cartoon cinema on the corner of Coventry Street and Shaftesbury Avenue. You know what men are like, if a woman sits alone they soon sidle up. I would accommodate them by hand in between rows A and B at the front. They never groaned, nor bothered to catch their emissions in tissues. I'd have hated to be a cleaner there, as the backs of most seats were caked up!

The fashion then was skinny-rib polo-neck, sleeveless sweaters, short skirts and boots. Doreen and I bought new 'whoring' (non-crease, easy-to-get-off, easy-to-wash, drip-dry) outfits from C&A in Oxford Steet, and were ready for action. She was on the pill and didn't bother with condoms. But I hated taking tablets (I hardly ever took aspirin or other conventional drugs), so I rejected the pill and was determined to use condoms to avoid another pregnancy. Furthermore, I detested the pungent odour which semen left on my vagina. No matter how much I bathed or douched after sex with the Duke, that horrid smell lingered for days.

In the late sixties, possession of 'French letters' as they were called was used against a woman as evidence of prostitution. Because of this I was too scared to carry them around and I relied on the client having some. If he didn't have any I'd urge him to buy some from Piccadilly's late-night chemist or use the machines in public toilets. (Later, when I was older and wiser, I patronised a shop at the south end of Wardour Street which specialised in supplying cut-price condoms, wigs and perfume to the 'trade'. I purchased fifty gross of condoms at a time.) On brave days I would work with three or four condoms concealed down my boots, but it made me nervous and I'd eventually lose my confidence to solicit. There was no reason then for a woman to be carrying condoms – this was before AIDS – so condoms, in the eyes of the law, represented soliciting, particularly if you had more than one on you! Doreen caught gonorrhoea and vaginal warts, but I was lucky.

However I did foolishly get tempted to have sex without a condom, and fell pregnant. I'm highly fertile, just like my mother and grandmother, and whenever I had sex without a condom I conceived immediately. I couldn't keep this baby, not after what I'd been through in France. My reasons were still the same: I was too young and hardly living a suitable life for motherhood. My predicament brought back painful memories of my son; I had awful morning sickness, all day long. I went off my favourite foods, and developed a craving for stews and dumplings.

An 'unwanted pregnancy' ad led me to the Pregnancy Advisory Bureau in Oxford Street. They sent me to two doctors (in those days you needed the consent of two) and then on to an abortion clinic. It cost me £150, and was an awful experience which I'll never forget. It was just like a cattle market: along with nineteen other spewing pregnant girls I was herded into a lift and taken up several floors to a ward. There I was shaved and told to wear a sanitary belt with clean towel hanging in readiness to be hooked into place afterwards. I continually vomited. The clock said 7 o'clock and four faces peered down at me from behind green masks. They gave me gas, and the next thing I remember was a fierce smarting sensation down below. I was elated to be rid of that non-stop nausea. The service was extremely bad: I was discharged after a few hours, without any medical monitoring. Later I heard that some of the doctors had been struck off.

I returned to whoring, and to 'mask' my vocation I got a straight job working as an usherette at the Odeon and then as a booking agent in the Empire cinema at Leicester Square. This gave me a legitimate reason to troll [walk about] through Soho at night. When apprehended I had a *bona-fide* excuse and could get all indignant: 'Do you mind, I'm on my way home from work!' I could have condoms on me and say they were for private use with my boyfriend – how dare they ask! Having those jobs allayed any suspicion, but they never lasted long. I always got bored and wanted better things.

I heard that some cabbies hired out the backs of their taxis and cruised around Regent's Park ignoring the business transaction in the back. I tried this tactic for a while. Then I moved on to picking up punters in cars and taking them to a lovers' lane by the river at Chiswick. It was a bit of a drive, about fifteen minutes from Soho, and by the time I reached Harrods they were concerned as to where I was taking them. I kept reassuring them, 'Next corner.' 'Just a little further. It'll be worth it.' This Chiswick haunt became popular with whores, and one night I met nine colleagues and two regular clients there.

By now my bed-sits had improved and for a while I lived in a large terraced house in Bounds Green, North London. I had a single room for £3 per week, but I sneaked Doreen in and made her pay half. From there we had easy access to lorry drivers along the North Circular Road for business, and we could get a lift into the West End to our respective beats. Once, as we were thumbing a lift, we got picked up by a squad car. The coppers called us 'a couple of Toms', which was the first time I'd heard the term 'Tomming' (derived from tom cats out on the prowl). We were let off with a caution.

If we had a good night we came home by taxi. Often I returned alone because Doreen liked to boogie all night in the drinking clubs, but I liked my sleep! I'd sneak in so as not to disturb the landlady, but her husband who was a dirty old sod stayed up making model airplanes and always hovered outside my room. I could see the shadows of his feet under the door. I teased him, flashing myself accidentally-on-purpose every time I went to the bathroom. I would have 'had it off' with him, but before I had the opportunity, his wife threw me out for raiding her refrigerator.

When I was soliciting the streets, I tried to avoid quick bunk-ups down alleys because they were cold and uncomfortable. Most men are a good deal taller than me – I'm short, 5 foot 4 inches – which means our genitalia are miles apart and I find it difficult to have sex standing up. If I wear high-heeled shoes my ankles give way under the strain, causing me to fall over. Gradually I discovered the perfect place for open-air work. There was a lovely smooth tarmac roof, comfortable to lie on, on a large Victorian block called Sandringham Flats opposite Leicester Square Tube in Charing Cross Road. It was the ideal sex spot. Several fire escapes facilitated disappearing acts, should cops or janitors come snooping round, and numerous tall chimney stacks radiated warmth from open fires.

In Soho, the going rate at the time was £4 – easy. But like most girls, I varied the prices according to my mood, predicament and the weather. Most of the local punters were Chinese, Greeks, Maltese and Indians, and some would bait me down to £3. If the vice squad were patrolling I'd accept a lesser sum just to get off the patch. I was amused to learn from first-hand experience that on average Chinese men have the smallest cocks. They are followed by Indians, another small race. And it's a common misconception that Negroes have the biggest penises. This is untrue! I agree that, compared to white men, their cocks look massive when flaccid. But they hardly grow when hard. A Caucasian penis grows two or three times from 'soft' to 'hard', making black and white men about the same. I've also noticed that thin men have bigger cocks than fat men. Fat men are the most troublesome fucks, as they have too much belly and it gets in the way; they are also so heavy that you can't breathe underneath them. Even doing it on top of them is awkward because you need your legs so far apart to straddle their wide bodies that you can't balance or manoeuvre properly. I refuse to accept fat men. My favourite clients are over 6 foot 4 inches and lean. I've a passion for really tall men and give them free extras.

Contrary to what a lot of people think, most street prostitutes get on together reasonably well. Naturally there's always a bit of bitching, but there is in any job. We would look out for each other, spreading the word if the police were around, and we all accepted that there were enough clients for everybody. One who wanted a tall leggy girl wouldn't come to me, nor would one who fancied a brunette. Likewise, men who wanted a bubbly blonde with giant bosoms wouldn't go to the others. When the weather was fine, on a Sunday, Doreen and I would meet other whores for a picnic in Hyde Park. We did lots of business in the bushes and behind trees, and there was a man who went around doing a roaring trade in condoms. We called him the 'French letter' man. We'd all be running around between punters looking for him!

When we finished at dusk I'd look for tourists in Park Lane. I targeted Arabs in particular because they ate a lot and I wanted to be wined and dined in posh hotel restaurants. On these occasions I ordered huge meals: T-bone steak, Brussels, cauliflower cheese and boiled potatoes, followed by trifle and cream, then Cheddar cheese and crackers. (The rampant sex afterwards burnt off the calories.) My overseas clients taught me to say 'You must wear a condom' in several languages. I've always liked to eat well and at the end of my work shift I would meet up with Doreen and my other colleagues in a café in Berwick Street called the Coffee Pot. There, unbeknownst to the staff or owners, people used to smoke weed or sniff amyl nitrate. I would eat sausage sandwiches and drink banana milkshakes.

We'd sit and unwind, chatting girl's talk just like anyone else: popular records, fashions, local boys we fancied. Maybe not so common was what we said about the corrupt police. We called them Lillians, short for 'Lilly Law', and female cops were called 'Judys' (because we wanted to 'punch' their faces in – 'Punch and Judy'). I heard many stories about cops who took cash or sex from girls in return for 'turning a blind eye', but I never experienced it myself until much later.

Afterwards we moved on to late-night clubs in D'Arblay Street or Wardour Mews. There were lots of doorways displaying 'Model' signs with red lights outside. For some reason I've always been drawn to the debauched atmosphere of sleazy alleys; I absolutely adore the night darkness. (In fact I can see better in the dark than I can in bright daylight.) I like the sparkle of stars against the black sky. I frequently lingered outside these knocking shops thinking 'One day I'll have a place like that.' However, inside the clubs I let my hair down in a different direction and did 'the grind' (an intimate, vulgar dance of the times) with junkies, lesbians, homosexuals, crooks, and blacks. We were one big happy family of social outcasts.

I still spent some time with the Hell's Angels. I liked jumping in and out of roles. I was out with them in full leathers at the Ace Café on the North Circular Road when a journalist from the *Observer* arrived. He was doing an article on 'teenage rebellion' and homed in on me because I looked so outrageous. I told him a load of bullshit, because he paid me £15, and I wanted to give him value for money. By the time the article appeared in the Sunday colour supplement, in April 1970, I was working straight at Rank film distributors (another ruse to mask my secret prostitution activities). I'd always kept in touch with my parents, even though I lied about my whereabouts, and on the whole, I had kept them satisfied and free from worry. But giving them my true location in this instance proved to be a mistake because my outraged father telephoned my work place. Another office junior answered the phone and said: 'There's someone for you with a sexy voice.'

My father came on the line: 'You dirty slag, don't you ever come to this house again.' He hung up.

I wasn't going there anyway, so I didn't care, but it upset me for a few hours. I wrote to him ten years ago condemning him for turning his back on me. In reply he wrote, amongst other things, that if he condoned my work then he would be no better than my punters.

The *Observer* article, accompanied by photographs, attracted a lot of attention which led to some modelling work with the Pretty Ugly agency in Charlotte Street. I did a modelling session at a studio dressed as a typical Hell's Angel mama, in denim jeans, a black wet-look blouse, belt made from a motorcycle chain, denim jacket with tattered edges and embroidered badges saying things like 'All coppers are bastards', 'Live hard – die young', 'The family that fucks together, stays together' and the proverbial 'Born to be wild'. I even had tattoos drawn on my face, arms and knuckles, and carried a fake machine gun wrapped in an old army blanket. I looked the business, which is why I was suddenly so sought after.

A record company in Carlisle Street, Soho, approached me, wanting me to be another Janis Joplin. My taste in music had always been Duane Eddy, Jerry Lee Lewis, Bill Haley, Del Shannon and French stuff. I didn't know who Janis Joplin was, but I went along to a studio in Blackbird Hill, North London for a demo. Unfortunately, my mistake was to choose an ambitious song – 'Ready Teddy' – which was very fast with a difficult range of high and low notes. Feedback came through my microphone which made me nervous, and my voice wobbled. They said I was tone deaf! I'm a good singer really, but on this occasion I got stage fright and made a total hash of my chance to be on *Top of the Pops*.

After that I hung out with Carole, a record plugger I'd met in a pub. She took me along to sex orgies with various popular DJs. I preferred this sort of game. It came so naturally to me and I was paid well, not for sex, but for my silence – something else I was good at!

My father rented a furnished flat in Olympia to ease the strain of commuting from Swindon to London for his job at the casino. He started speaking to me again, but the atmosphere was strained. My sister was still the apple of his eye and I was the family's 'black sheep'. My mother got bored alone in Wiltshire, so she moved to London as well. They rented a three-bedroomed house in Stratford, which came in handy because I got fed up with small bed-sits, and persuaded my parents to put me up while I looked for a self-contained flat. Old habits didn't die, and when my parents were out at work, I picked up clients from Lea Bridge Road by the edge of Epping Forest and sneaked them into the house. I serviced them on my parents' bed. I lay there wondering what would happen if they came home unexpectedly!

After a couple of weeks I found a furnished flat on the ground floor of a large Victorian house in Perham Road, West Kensington, where I could take my clients at my leisure. It was extremely well placed, in a tiny cul-de-sac with a clear view of everyone approaching. There was a phone box outside so clients could check I was available. (Some clients get embarrassed when there's a full house: they don't want to be seen by other men, and most like to think they're 'the first'.) Immediately next door was an entrance to a well-known centre for tennis players, Queen's Club. I could lure in prominent sportsmen. The flat was £16 per week and I moved in with my entire estate – the contents of which fitted inside a black taxi!

There was easy access to work from West Kensington Tube, which was a few minutes' walk. I took the tube to Green Park and worked a better quality 'beat' comprising Half Moon Street (the east side of which was reserved for rent boys), left into Curzon Street, right into Park Lane and up to Marble Arch, then back again cutting through Hertford Street where I took a rest. A beautiful large period house there still retained its original coachman's porch complete with little oak seat. This was bliss for two reasons: firstly, to hide from the police when they took whores off to be charged; and secondly, to sit down and massage my throbbing toes which had been crammed into 6 inch stilettos and which had just walked three miles!

I noticed an established brothel at number 39 Curzon Street, Mayfair, which had a red neon light in the window saying 'French Lessons'. Through the ground-floor window passers-by could see two black leather high-back chairs conveniently positioned opposite one another. One had its back to the street so you couldn't see the person sitting there and various women alternately sat in full view faking conversation with the fictitious pupil opposite, but of course there was nobody there. This was a marvellous ruse to fool 'straight' people walking past into thinking a private conversation was occurring. Otherwise they might have taken offence and complained to the authorities. Any interested clients understanding that 'French lessons' meant oral sex simply rang the bell and enjoyed a 'lesson'. I often stood across the road watching enviously, wishing I could be inside such a forbidden place, but I kept my distance after hearing rumours it was run by two Maltese brothers who were notorious pimps.

In 1990 this house came on the open market with an asking price of one and a quarter million pounds. I put in a bid on behalf of a syndicate but was gazumped by developers. It is now a luxury office building.

Whilst soliciting I became aware of the ingenious ploys used by prostitutes to throw moralists and the police off their trail. One house in Shepherd's Street displayed a large framed portrait of the 'model' on the inside windowsill: this was arranged to look as if it had been accidentally knocked, thus was facing outwards instead of inwards. To fool the police, I often posed as a tourist window shopping, and it was through this that I found a shop in Edgware Road which sold uniforms. I considered it a good ruse to kit myself out in full nurse's regalia, and pretend I had just finished work at St George's Hospital at Hyde Park Corner. This had a double advantage because most men liked nurse fantasies, and I easily enticed them by saying 'Fancy a private medical, sir?'

When my uniform was being laundered, I reverted to my usual line of patter which had now expanded to 'Business! Nice time no rush.' I usually managed to get five clients a night. The only thing that bothered me was the enormous amount of time wasted hanging around in the wind and rain looking for clients, and travelling five miles to and from my flat. There weren't enough hours in the day or night to squeeze in any more. (At Madame's in Paris I had been able to receive ten clients within a ten-hour shift, working in the 'salon', and forty (one every fifteen minutes) whenever I worked the back rooms at the rear catering for cheap quickies.)

Whilst wearing my uniform on public transport, I was surprised at how much respect the public had for nurses. Often on the tube, people would offer me their seats. I always felt guilty accepting, but did so to rest my blistered feet (an occupational hazard of street-walking). Despite the popular misconception that a whore is on her back all the time, it's in fact her feet she's on, in crippling shoes which we called 'Killer Morillas'.

On another occasion I was trolling along Knightsbridge, when the Vice Squad pulled up. My heart missed a beat, and I expected to be nicked, but my disguise fooled them completely. They thought I had finished night shift and offered to drive me home. It took all my acting ability to present a serious medical image (I was wearing a smart blue Sister's uniform with a frilly cap): I invented imaginary patients and fictitious medicines to keep a plausible conversation going until I reached my destination.

During this 'medical' period, I had a scare when a drunken motorist picked me up outside Harrods. I got into his Bentley to discuss terms when he suddenly sped off like a maniac. My hitch-hiking days had taught me how to jump out of moving vehicles as they slowed at corners or traffic signals, but in this instance he didn't observe the highway code and clearly took pleasure in frightening me.

'Look! I'm needed on duty to save somebody's life. You've got to let me out.'

I stood up to him because evil men are like animals: they can smell fear and this makes them ten times more nasty. When he skidded to a halt I fled.

After this unpleasant experience I decided to get off the streets. I installed a telephone at home in order to operate as a call-girl. My homosexual friends had kept in touch and a Scottish transvestite called Lulu agreed to work as my maid (someone to usher men in and out) and double up as a minder (to get rid of troublesome clients). She (I always refer to trannies as 'she') wore my nurse's outfit to look neat and crisp, and she touted by the green iron railings of the Queen's Club entrance. She gave anyone entering or leaving the club my newly printed business cards which bore the line, 'The Best in the West' and my phone number. From my window I provocatively displayed my wares from underneath a transparent black nylon baby-doll nightie. I sprang into action the moment a likely client showed interest: 'Hey, darling! Let me play with your balls. Come inside for some fun.' The fees ranged from 5 guineas up to 100 for all night. (I liked guineas – they sounded posher!)

Whenever I had a good day, I treated Lulu, who was an alcoholic, to drinking binges at West End hotels, and I'd solicit at the same time. My favourite bars for this practice were in the Regent Palace in Piccadilly, the Cumberland at Marble Arch and the Hilton in Mayfair.

It was in the Regent Palace that I met John, a sixty-year-old man who headed a well-established firm of solicitors. He was actually on his way to Liverpool Street Station after visiting the Earl's Court Boat Show, but fancied chatting about boats and stopped off for a drink. I wanted to talk about sex and offered myself for £25. He baited me down to £12.50, paying by cheque, and became the bargain of my life. First we dined at the Carvery (it cost £2.75 in those days), then we went to my flat for straight sex. Our friendship blossomed, and was to span many years. Through 'swopsies', he took care of future conveyancing and various legal problems, and I looked after his sex drive. He liked my nurse's uniform and sometimes I wore it to visit his office. We had sex on his desk, knocking all his clients' files on to the floor, and afterwards at his request I caned his bottom with a walking stick.

I became his sounding board as he confided all his problems to me. His wife had died and on the rebound he had married his housekeeper: he paid her a settlement and she moved out; he was lonely. He became my main regular client, and wrote me love letters every day. (I still have them.) Sometimes he took me to his rambling detached house in Essex (after his children had gone to bed). We also visited his holiday homes and went out on his boat. He promised to leave money for me in his will, but I expect someone persuaded him otherwise.

Unfortunately our relationship came to an acrimonious end. Many years afterwards, John's son, who had always resented our friendship, entered the firm and took over my file. He threatened to send me a bill for all the work his father had previously carried out. I was furious and sent John 'my' bill – £10,000 for sexual services and escort duties. The matter was never raised again, but it soured my friendship with John and I dumped him.

I had many regulars – all tit lovers – and one of them picked up a whore called Charlotte in the Cumberland Hotel and brought her along for a lesbian scene. We became friends – she'd been one of Madame's girls in Paris – and she introduced me to other 'hotel girls'. I teamed up with eleven others who regularly worked the bars, and we became so notorious that the concierges and local journalists looking for a scoop called us 'The Dirty Dozen'. Sometimes it was possible to bribe hotel managers to turn a blind eye in return for 25 per cent commission.

For this game I wore my favourite Frank Usher evening gowns, mink wraps and costume jewellery, and I developed a gimmick of standing outside the glitzy entrances holding a box of chocolates or a bouquet as if I was waiting for my partner to park the car. However, my distinctive ensemble was easy to recognise and the Vice Squad soon cottoned on. On the same night they captured me once outside the Hilton, twice in Hereford Street, and a third time outside the BMW shop in Park Lane. After the third caution I was whisked off for hospitality at Her Majesty's pleasure – a night in a stinking cold police cell. The following morning I was fined £1 at Bow Street court. The magistrate looked over his half glasses at me and said: 'We take a very grim view of this. Don't let me see you before me again!'

Determined to prosper, I placed my first advert in a shop window along North End Road, West Kensington. A small white card with 'Private Stylist, Lorelie Lanvin'. I took the name Lorelie from Marilyn Monroe's character in *Gentlemen Prefer Blondes*; the surname, Lanvin, came from a well-known brand of perfume. The terminology 'stylist' could be taken for 'hairdressing', so I felt confident when handing it to the shopkeeper. Rejection of stronger cards was an embarrassment I didn't care for. A little later I got bolder and had 'Private Lessons by Miss Sabrina' printed on fancy blue cards with gold crinkly edging. The name Sabrina was taken from a popular actress with large breasts.

Lulu left my employment so I started to work on my own. As a safety precaution I taped male and female voices and ferociously barking dogs, and left the tape playing in another room to give my client the illusion that I wasn't alone. Every now and again my visitor heard: 'Chain that bloody dog up!' and 'Has Sabrina finished yet?' I had to make sure the client stayed less than a hour otherwise the tape repeated, and my game was up.

Within a few weeks my new card got noticed by the Vice Squad, but thanks to Jake's instruction of 'See everything, hear everything', I was one step ahead – watching them watching me! Their squad car was supposedly hidden round the corner, but I could see their rear bumper. They knew I was in, but I ignored them as various plain-clothes detectives repeatedly knocked at my door. Then they went to the phone box and rang my number. I heard them curse me: 'Fucking bitch. We'll get her tomorrow.'

It was time to go! My rent was paid until the end of the month, so I left my stuff behind and checked into the Regent Palace Hotel where, as a guest, I could solicit the bars without reproach. I still walked the streets in Mayfair and Soho, sometimes loitering by telephone boxes and relieving clients inside. A friend told me about a posh hairdresser in Knightsbridge who sold bent massage diplomas for £10 and a wank, so I got one as a ruse to set up in another flat as a *bona-fide* masseuse. Then if I was raided, I could do my indignant bit and say: 'Do you mind! I'm a qualified masseuse.'

It is illegal for property owners to allow their premises to be used for prostitution, so rather than be nicked for 'living off immoral earnings', 'procuring' or 'aiding and abetting', landlords (apart from bent ones) refused then to accept single female tenants. However, there were bent estate agents who specialised in rentals to whores at a premium of double the rent plus key money. My friend Anne had such a 'bent' flat in Trebeck Street, Mayfair, at £800 a week (probably the equivalent of £3,000 today). I begrudged greedy agents, and decided to front up a gay man in order to secure a rental agreement on a 'straight' flat. I had two weeks to find a suitable one, preferably in a basement with its own entrance.

I'd learned a lot in the past few years, but while I was beginning to be my own person, in charge of my own fate, my connection with Jake had not been severed. During my time 'on the game' in London I'd made several trips back to France, both to spend time with him and for brief working holidays at Madame's. I had ambition and enthusiasm, and grew increasingly tired of street-walking, bed-sits and flats. In my search for success and prosperity, I compared myself to traders of 'specialist' merchandise who start off small and evolve into multi-national chain stores. That's what I wanted! The next step up the prostitution ladder was to run a brothel of my own!

5

Coming Up Market

My ambition was to build as good a reputation as Madame in Paris. Her clients were protected by her discretion. Since in England brothels were neither acceptable nor legal places of business, I would have to be even more careful. I inspected several furnished flats before I decided on one in Trebovir Road, Earls Court. It had the additional attraction of another vacant flat on an upper floor which I could use as private living-quarters. This too was fully furnished. The flat I would use as my brothel had French windows leading to a garden bordering Templeton Place. My clients would have a fast and shielded exit if necessary. It was a 'straight' flat, and I 'bent' it.

At this stage, I also took on what was to be my final last name. I'd nicked Linda off a girl at school I'd had a crush on. But a lot of my Arab clients couldn't say 'Linda', so it became Lindi. Now, as a last name, I tried to decide between St Claire, St James, Du Barry, Du Pont or Van Heusen. Since I liked the book *Forever Amber* and identified with the heroine's era, I took her name, St Claire. (Several years later, a client pointed out to me that the anagram of St Claire was 'Clit arse', so I immediately dropped the 'e'! Although I was a whore, I was a lady and I didn't want to be associated with anything that vulgar.)

The ground-floor flat was spacious and could be adapted to what I had in mind. The large living room led at one end to a bedroom, and at the other to a kitchen and bathroom. The actual bedroom was small, so I kept that for anyone who wanted complete privacy. The living room was then divided in half with a curtain, to make two 'rooms'.

My good fortune at that time was to hire a maid who was experienced. Flora had worked for other prostitutes and claimed she had a patter that would have men drooling in the phone boxes when they called. It did, her routine always ensuring a prompt arrival, and I have passed it on to many girls since. (Sadly, Flora was to let me down in the end. She took liberties with my money which was a shame because our relationship started out so well.)

Flora had a husky, sensual voice designed to excite the male. When a call came in, she went into action: 'Measurements, 39½, 24, 38' (my bosoms constantly fluctuated according to weight gains or losses; they had reduced to 40, and Flora felt 39½ sounded more sexy) – pause – 'nice legs' – longer pause – 'marvellous equipment' – with emphasis – 'special rooms'.

To those in the know, this meant kinky. The word 'special' in the trade means deviations, and for this you needed appropriate props. When I had my first request for spanking, I had to hunt around the flat for something suitable. I used the fish slice from the kitchen drawer! When asked for bondage, I'd have to improvise with my dressing-gown cord or plimsoll laces. Men who wanted to wear ladies' underwear – transvestites – would borrow mine. And when one man said he wanted nipple clamps, the bulldog clips from my writing desk were called into service. Flora advised me where to buy proper equipment and sent me, for instance, to a place in Richmond called Weather Vane for rubberwear. This was known as 'rainwear' in the trade and I often wondered what the local ladies might have made of the shop if they popped in for an umbrella on a rainy day . . . .

A few prostitutes had a room put aside for these special services, but I had no real space. That men could require that sort of humiliation was beyond belief to me, but . . . business is business. I started to take their needs into consideration and, amongst other things, I fixed up a cupboard in the hall with a hook at each of the four corners so that a man could be spread-eagled behind the closed door. These 'indulgences' were charged as an extra over the basic rate, then £1 a minute. Later, I had a small torture rack made which stood against the wall in the little bedroom. I was quite willing to play these games. It was good fun, bringing out the best in my creative nature. Not only was this an easier way to earn money, but dressing up and acting appealed to me. I had a devoted, grateful audience, and I was centre stage.

Flora advised me to work from 10 am to 7 pm. 'The early bird catches the worm.' I saw several advantages in this. After 7 pm my neighbours, who were all straight, would be home from work, and there was less likelihood of complaints if they were not disturbed by my visitors. The upmarket men that I wanted as clients were solid family men who daren't be out late anyway. They would be clean and smart and treat my 'house' with respect, not wanting any ripples across the pond of their private lives. In addition, running during the day eliminated the evening trade, single men who were mainly scruffy, drunk and troublesome.

I spread the word about my establishment in top-shelf contact magazines. I regularly went into newsagents to check them and was always amused at the way the men who were browsing there scattered at my approach. As a back-up, I put cards on the news-agents' boards as well, and also had the bright idea of writing my phone number on every pound note I handled: 'Model – phone number' brought in at least 30 per cent of my customers.

I assembled a dozen girls from among colleagues from the street and hotel scene. We would sit around in one half of the living room, eating, drinking and watching the TV. The flat could hold five men, and we'd play 'musical rooms': as one man left the bedroom, the next in the queue, who might have been waiting in the kitchen or bathroom, took his place. The average time of a quickie or hand service was four minutes, so no-one had long to wait, and they were raring to go anyway!

I also employed a minder to eject nuisance clients and keep an eye on proceedings. He spent his time up in my private flat connected to us by an intercom system. I planned to operate under similar rules to the brothel in Paris. I paid for the advertising which was mostly cards in newsagents' windows. Men who came along were allo-cated the first girl on the rota, the second client had the next girl and so on, so that each whore got her fair share of clients. However, some girls also placed independent adverts stating they were avail-able on my number. Anyone responding to their ads, asking for them by name, was deemed their personal client regardless of her place on the list.

The men paid their fees to me, which I split 50–50 with the girls. My responsibility, besides advertising, was to supply the premises, protection, advice on health and sexual services, kinky equipment, food and drink. I provided a running buffet in the kitchen with champagne, smoked salmon and other delicacies delivered daily by Harrods. (I had accounts by then with all the big stores, but Harrods was the closest for food.) I also supplied condoms. I've always had a house rule that condoms must be used. I'm fanatical about it.

I kept another of Madame's rules and took the girls to church on Sundays! We went either to the church in Philbeach Gardens or the one in Earl's Court Road. No-one objected; they were grateful to be working in a warm brothel as opposed to braving the elements out on the street.

I had a problem with some of them over the condom rule. One or two cheated. It was the same old story: they'd been tempted by men who would pay extra if a condom wasn't used. They were found out because Flora was so fastidious. Her theory was that the room had to be immaculate for each man. She went in after each client, sprayed the room to perfume the air, and tidied up. She was quick to notice if there were only tissues in the waste-bin. I then kept an eye on the girl and double-checked with the client when next we spoke. They were always honest with me. If he said he hadn't used a condom, I would tell him off and warn him that if she'd chanced it once, one had to assume she'd done it with other men before him. He was therefore running the risk of disease. The client was warned he would be barred if he did this again – and I did have to bar some. The girl was instantly sacked.

Some of the clients were company chairmen who arrived before or after board meetings. Their chauffeurs often had a girl as well as a tip. It was all very matey. There was plenty of money coming in – in fact I was earning a fortune – and it went into several bank accounts. Some of the managers were impressed enough to become friends and clients too!

One afternoon, my minder was watching from the upstairs window and saw two police cars parking. He rushed down to tell me that six officers were approaching. We had less than five minutes head-start to get rid of the evidence: clients, girls, condoms and the small props. I transformed the rack with some pots of trailing ivy while everyone else ran out of the back way into the garden and over the walls. Some were still in party gear; one transvestite was still wearing stockings and suspenders. Fortunately around that area, someone dressed like that could hail a cab without comment.

I was waiting in my lounge, building up a steam of indignation, when the police busted the door off its hinges. They found me, legs crossed provocatively, sipping champagne.

'My, my, you are in a hurry. Fancy a drink?'

'You're nicked, love.'

Underlings went in all directions looking for evidence – and found nothing. They came back and said to me: 'Ha, ha, very clever.' But the word of the police is taken in such cases without any evidence, so the one in charge said: 'Don't give us any extra paperwork, plead guilty. Pay your fine – it's just like paying tax – and go back to work.'

They didn't care, they'd had their pat on the back for being 'good' cops. This was my first brothel-keeping offence, and I was heavily fined. The police grassed to the landlord and he gave me notice to quit. I had paid two weeks' rent in advance, so I had time to make new arrangements. During this time Jake phoned. He knew I'd been nicked, as the family were still keeping tabs on me. He made sure that I was all right, then he proposed marriage and suggested we pick up on the promises we'd made when he was in hospital – like having a baby of our own.

I needed time to think. Did he really mean it? I had to consider it all very carefully. Here I was at the age of twenty, doing extremely well on my own. I'd made a life for myself. For instance a couple of years earlier, in my constant quest for something 'new', I'd gone on an expensive cruise; outside boat deck, double-bedded cabin, a sort of working holiday. I could look out of my window and twinkle at the men jogging past. I had enough responses to be able to gamble away a lot of money playing 'joker seven', a card game unique to cruise ships. Enthusiastic prostitutes like myself often travel far afield on working holidays to where clients *en masse* can be found. For example, we flock to international events like the Cannes Film Festival, Monaco's Grand Prix, Australia's Gold Cup, and wherever the Olympic Games are (I book my hotel accommodation a year in advance). In Britain, I especially enjoy hanging out at Blackpool during the Tory conference, and at posh hotels where delegates stay. There are always businessmen who get lonely and randy whilst away from home, and they're easily enticed into paying for sex.

Jake's proposition left me torn between taking a chance on this marriage, having our baby at long last, or continuing to take care of myself. While trying to make up my mind, though, life had to go on.

Firstly I had to move. I found a flat in the nearby Old Brompton Road, but in order not to be recognised for what I was, I had a homosexual friend front for me by paying the deposit. Then, with a client who had now become a friend, we trundled my belongings, including the rack, down the Earl's Court Road on a barrow borrowed from a fruit vendor. (Later, this client worked at Kensington Palace, where I was able to frolic on Queen Victoria's bed!)

Again, rather than pay a ridiculously high rent, this was a 'straight' flat. My girls had been scared off by the raid, so I carried on alone for a while. Landlords rarely lived on the premises, but one day mine knocked. I thought he was a punter and kept buzzing the intercom to let him in. He thought it was peculiar that I hadn't asked who he was first and this confirmed his suspicion that I was no ordinary tenant. He had been watching, and told me he had seen around sixty men come and go with the maid showing them in and out like an usherette in a cinema. I suggested paying him double the rent in order to stay, because there was a great potential for business in this flat, but he wanted me out. I was only there a month (the few props I had, I threw away).

I decided to go to Paris and give Jake another chance. Besides promising marriage, he had also said he would retire. But this wasn't to be. He was caught up in the merry-go-round of his underworld life. When he came home one night with a contract on which he would make a million francs, I was appalled at the details. It was too dreadful – too big a secret for me to keep and stay with him. I saw it would be better for me to cut loose completely. Our relationship – which had gone on for seven years – was at an end. Much as I loved him, I had to accept it was over.

To make the break permanent, I went to Switzerland and cleared the account which had held my earnings from my time in the Paris brothel. I took nothing from the joint account but left a note: 'See everything, hear everything, say nothing.' This was my way of reassuring him that his secrets were safe with me. The family continued to keep an eye on me from then on and knew I kept my mouth shut.

I removed my stash of cash and jewellery from under the floor-boards off the Paris flat, and cleaned the place thoroughly to remove any evidence I had been there. Dressed in the best Paris fashion, I boarded the London-bound plane, where I tripped on my stilettos into the arms of the man who was to be my seat mate. Full of apologies, I flirted madly. He turned out to be in the film world and a frequent traveller. He offered me his card with the usual line: 'Anything I can do for you, give me a call.'

Sitting there with all my cash and jewellery stuffed into my pantie girdle, I saw a chance to get through Customs without any hassle and confessed to him I had an excess of valuables on my person. We walked out through the Green Channel arm in arm and parted outside the airport with promises to meet again.

My first stop was the Savoy. I swept in and booked a suite. This would be my base while I investigated the property market. I now had the money to buy something really spectacular, and I started to comb the property lists. I found places that fitted what I had in mind in Curzon Street, Montpelier Square and, amusingly for me, Meard Street, Soho, where I had once lurked. That young, somewhat naïve girl was someone I now hardly knew. I had a purpose in my life and was determined to be a successful Madam.

An estate agent came round to take me on an inspection tour. I told him I wanted to have the best whorehouse in London. Shocked but agreeable – after all, he saw a fat commission – he was ready to help. Our first stop was a mansion in Cheyne Walk which had belonged to a peer who died in 1960. It was now derelict, but I could see great potential in the massive oak-panelled reception hall and curved sweep of staircase. All it needed was a lot of money spent on it. I told the estate agent I was keen to bring this building back to its former glory. The owners didn't seem to agree with my ideas because I was telephoned with the news that it was with another agent and now under offer.

I looked at several more places with different agents, not realising that Earl's Court was still exerting its influence on me until I was sent details of a house in Eardley Crescent. I felt I had come home. It was perfect for a brothel. The place was freehold, with vacant possession of the basement and ground floor. It was spacious, and the rooms could be divided without any problem. There was a back way out into the next street (very important for avoiding unwelcome guests like the Vice Squad), and a roof for a look-out point and as another escape route. It was three seconds from Earl's Court Tube and at the end of a terrace, so there were no neighbours on the left. The adjoining hallways on the right meant that my neighbours there would not be disturbed by visitors indulging in a little more than the pleasure of my whores' company. . . . Oh, I'd learned a lot about men's requirements by now and planned to accommodate them with straight *and* kinky sex. The underground basement would make an excellent dungeon.

I paid £17,500 out of the bank account I'd opened in the Earl's Court Road. There was a lot of work ahead. The house had suffered from multiple occupancy, and there was damp and woodworm. I had to take a flat in nearby Philbeach Gardens in order to oversee all that needed to be done. My personal quarters would be on the ground floor, with a private entrance. Harrods came in to do the furnishing – no expense spared. I had mirrored walls, velvet drapes, gilt-trimmed rosewood furniture, and chandeliers. I wanted it to scream money in the same way that Jake's flat in Paris had done. When I was ready to start, I felt marvellous. I knew I had a money-spinner here.

Now I was ready to advertise for staff. Not only in kinky magazines and on cards but, suitably adjusted, in the local papers and *The Lady*. I wanted to get a full selection of people.

> 'Young ladies required to work in new, central London, upmarket gentlemen's club. All levels of employment offered – hostess, maid, cook, masseuse, seamstress, wardrobe mistress, governess, barmaid, waitress and chauffeur. Top wages and fabulous fringe benefits.'

Hundreds of women telephoned and wrote for interviews. Some were innocents in search of a genuine job. A young woman who was a maid at Sandringham hoped to improve on her position! Men who applied to be chauffeurs were rejected. I only wanted female staff. I was spoilt for choice. In the end, I decided to interview *en masse* and took a suite in a West End hotel. About a hundred turned up. It was standing room only. I made a speech explaining the scene and invited those who wanted to leave to do so immediately and not waste anyone's time. A few shuffled out in shock. I asked those who had come to apply as domestic staff to remain while the future whores went down to the bar to wait for an hour. It was necessary to do it in this order – the domestic staff would have lost their nerve if asked to wait.

My methods worked. In the vice world, your staff become your friends, so I chose the best spoken, most presentable girls, who seemed to be on the same wavelength as me. They also had to be tall. As I was short, I always needed people to pass me down things from shelves, and there were floor-to-ceiling shelves all round the house in Eardley Crescent. An extra attraction for me was the girls who, like me, were into keeping fit and swimming. They could keep me company at a local health club after working hours. The whores came back next. My requirements were not the same for them. I needed ten very different looking women; black, white, tall, short, fat, thin, busty, flat-chested, young, old, blonde, brunette. They all had to strip off. Any ugly operation scar was rejected, as was a bad skin condition. I found one with tattoos, who would make the perfect slut with greasy hair and laddered stockings. This disproves the popular misconception – men do *not* need to kerb-crawl for a slut. You can get them in a brothel!

Once I had staff and whores, I needed clients. It was back to Harrods to buy books like *Debrett's, Who's Who?, Prominent British Families* and *The World's Top 500 Richest People*. I was looking for upper-crust clients. Madame had always got between 3 and 5 per cent response from her mail-shots, so expecting the same, I sent out 5,000 invitations.

'Join Madeleine du Bon from Paris. Now known as Lindi St Clair. Grand opening party. Eat, drink and be merry with any woman of your choice. Safe, Clean, Discreet. No charge. RSVP.'

Opening night coincided with my twenty-third birthday. I paid for the party: £5,000 for food, drink, entertainment, printing and postage. The food was set up in my private lounge, a big table with large joints of turkey, ham and beef. Some of my transvestite customers dressed up as maids and carved with huge knives. More than 200 guests turned up and mingled with the girls, who had been paid by me for the night. They were told to screw the punters' brains out and give them a good time. They were forbidden to ask for money, as everything was on the house. They were promised a long-term job if they obeyed the rules of the house, not to gossip and to be discreet. I was determined to follow all I had learned from Madame in Paris.

No-one was allowed into the party without an invitation. Men were handed a ski mask as they arrived, to wear in case they wanted to hide their identity. Everyone accepted them as a novelty along with a condom and stick-on badge inscribed either, 'straight', 'voyeur', or 'submissive'. This meant they did not need to indulge in conversation unless they chose. (Since then, I have bought ski masks by the gross because they get slobbered on and it's very unhygienic to use them again. Washing is equally useless; they shrink.)

The party was a great success. Following arrows that said 'sex this way', guests and girls began to spill into various rooms. It was a hot evening and some went out in the back garden and up on the roof. Dozens of bouquets also arrived from randy men unable to make the party but asking to be informed of future events. I could see that I had a good thing going.

It continued that way. Punters would phone to say they were bringing friends. I'd get in extra girls and supplies as necessary. One tycoon, Robert Maxwell in fact, even brought some of his business associates along for 'free' sex (which he paid for) in order to clinch a deal. As my reputation grew, applications came in from people wanting to be part of the staff.

I carried on with the mail-shot idea too. Whenever I receive junk mail I usually throw it away, never opening it, unless it happens to arrive when I am bored. Only then do I take a look, and sometimes succumb and contact the sender. I thought men might react in the same way to unsolicited mail from a brothel.

First I needed a 'top-drawer' mailing list, so I created one by feeding my computer databank with the names, ages and locations of millionaires, royals, heads of state and politicians, all of which I gleaned from media sources. I was so meticulous about details that I couldn't read a newspaper without a pair of scissors handy to cut out articles and photographs. I watched the TV news with a notebook and pen. I even combed the electoral registers for addresses.

I made it my business to find out the hobbies and habits of prospective future clients so that I could periodically surprise them with sex brochures sent to various locations. For example, a peer who went riding was mail-shot at a Scottish equestrian centre; an MP's son who went disco-dancing received my brochure at a Somerset night club; and a member of the royal family got my details at Lydd Airport. Every birthday, Valentine's Day, Easter, Hallowe'en, Guy Fawkes Night and Christmas I sent both current and prospective clients saucy cards. The law of averages meant some would respond, and out of the thousands of multiple mail-shots I sent, 3 per cent replied, which I considered a good result.

Perhaps surprisingly, I also read the classified ads in *The Lady*. There are always names and locations of landed gentry when they

Top left: Me aged 2 (on the right), with my mother and older sister in our back garden in East London.

Top right: Age 7. At Swindon, posing for the annual Junior School portrait.

Right: Age 13, visiting the champagne cellars in Reims.

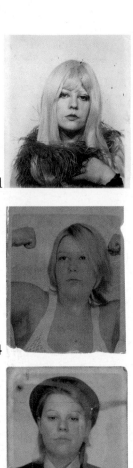

1

2

3

4

5

6

7

8

9

Snaps of me between the ages of 13 and 18 in London and Paris.

1. Soho stripper with feather boa.

2. Topless barmaid at a hostess club in St James's.

3. Gangster disguise, using Jake's father's clothes and cigar, Paris.

4. Working out with 'the boys' in Paris, string vest and all.

5. Delivering packages for 'the family'.

6. Teddy Boy disguise.

7. Gay boy disguise.

8. Housewife disguise.

9. My favourite look, a young, up-market Parisian whore.

Left: Wicked Queen Service. *'Eat my nice red juicy apple!'*

Above left: School Marm Service. *'Naughty boys get bottom marks.'*

Above right: Rubber Nun Service. *'And thou shalt worship no other Goddess but me.'* Syndication International

Right: Virgin Bride Wedding Night Service. *'I do.'*

Beside my automatic motorised rotation rack. *'Sinning while spinning.'*
  Syndication International

advertise for housekeepers, gamekeepers or butlers. If the particular aristocrat's name or rank isn't mentioned, I address my brochure to the 'Lord and Master of the House' and sent it to the relevant country estate. From this particular scam I have had an excellent success rate, the highest in fact of all my single mail-shot groups. Of 142 aristocrats repeatedly mail-shot, sixty-three responded within the first year. They all confessed to being bored stiff, with plenty of time and money to spare. But they are such pompous gits, and difficult to please, that I charge them an extra £50 'nuisance tax'!

The poorest response from my single mail-shot groups is from Brigadiers and Vice Admirals whom I contact at locations where they have dined. (I elicit these from newspaper reports.) Apart from the few I already had (who had found me by other means), in all, out of twenty-seven others repeatedly mail-shot, only one responded – a doddery old chap of about ninety who wanted straight sex, with me wearing black stiletto, thigh-length boots. During his service, he puffed like a train shunting to a halt, then he lay totally still. I thought he'd had a heart attack on the job, so I prodded him to see if he were still alive. He said, 'Sorry, poppet. I was just savouring the last few moments. I haven't done it for five long years.' He's the oldest man I've had sex with. I was surprised he had it in him!

My lists were updated monthly, and still are. Business and social addresses are amended accordingly, and those who die, as many have over the years, are deleted.

Ever with a view to the future, I keep a separate 'young-drawer' lists for clients' sons, and when they reach sixteen, they are transferred to the 'top-drawer' list. They are sent my 'School for Casanovas' mail-shot (sex lessons for willing beginners); sometimes I offer free and discounted prices to entice in those sons who repeatedly ignore me. Whilst I'm thorough with my research, it's not always possible to locate photographs of the sons whom I mail-shot, therefore when shy ones have visited me without announcing their names, I haven't recognised them. I was amused recently when an MP's son was undressing prior to a £30 service. He said: 'My dad would go mad if he knew I was here. He can't stand you.' 'Oh, really! Who's your dad then?' 'It's . . .' The feeling was mutual!

It surprised me how much young sons liked to defy, show off or gossip about their rich or famous fathers. I found adolescent boys to be easy pickings, especially when they were offered free sex. Quite a few older sons became regular clients and proved useful in providing me with otherwise unavailable political gossip, like which Cabinet Minister was screwing the wife of someone at the Foreign Office, or which of the Prime Minister's advisers was screwing one of the catering staff.

Another political son belonged to an anarchist group which opposes bureaucracy and private wealth, and strangely enough many rebellious offspring from prominent families are members. Apparently his father (whom I had frequently mail-shot during previous years) had recognised my envelope and confiscated it, thinking his son would be none the wiser. However, the seventeen year old had already spotted his mail on the doormat, but not bothered to pick it up. He confronted his father, demanded his mail, and ended up having a row, defending the rights of whores. He visited me for free sex (after being sent twelve brochures over two years without his father noticing). We had a good romp, then spent the whole day drinking cider and slagging off the system.

The funny thing was that his father, already one of my clients, was afraid his son would turn out as deviant as he. But such concern was uncalled for. His son was a red-blooded stud, hungry for straight sex with large-breasted ladies, not at all sado-masochistic like his father (who liked stinging nettles and lit sparklers applied to his erection).

Whether in response to mail-shots or my cards, there were always a few men who tried to get something for nothing. They are called 'bilkers' in the trade. They'd come to the door and be shown in by the maid. I received clients in a black basque and black stockings (Pretty Polly holdups).

Their questions followed a similar pattern.

'What do you do?'

'How much is it?'

Then the excuses.

'I've left my wallet in the car.'

'I'm on a parking meter.'

They had no intention of having a service and caused a problem. If you ran them off – told them to get lost, or were more explicit – the straight clients got a free ogle, and the kinky ones had been dominated – both having had a free service, which was exactly what they were after!

In spite of such pseudo customers, my brothel flourished until, in 1976, the *News of the World* exposed me. I was called 'the most evil woman in Britain', because I was catering for masochists. It appeared that they specialised in exposing prostitution, and one day Trevor Kempson, a *News of the World* journalist, paid £30 and came in for a service. Unbeknownst to me, he had a tape-recorder – I know this because the article quoted me word for word. On reflection, I should have sued for libel. My character was defamed. I consider murder, kidnapping and arson to be evil, but certainly not the consensual sex games which I was playing. They zoom-lensed in and sneaked a picture of me in my fancy dressing-gown putting out the milk bottles.

Shortly after that, it was my turn to be nicked again. The police had commandeered a room across the street which overlooked my entrance. The owner of this building was one of my customers, and he came and told me they were there. We went on red-alert and carried on, escape routes planned. We were watching them watching us. The norm for a police observation is three days, and during this time officers posed as clients (who 'bilked') to suss the place out. I had a temporary maid at that time. She had been warned that when the police knocked she should only speak to them through a side window. But when they arrived, she panicked at the sight of all the uniforms. She opened the door and they poured in.

Several of us managed to shout: 'It's a raid. All out!' Everyone escaped through the back exits, except, that is, for three men who were in bondage. I had five small fetish chambers available by then. A vicar was in one, wearing rubber boots and gas mask, handcuffed to the wall; a peer was in a straitjacket in a cupboard; and an MP was chained in the dog kennel in the garden.

By then, I was sitting in my lounge hearing those usual three words, 'You're nicked, love.' A police photographer accompanied them, and took pictures of every room. None of them could believe their eyes!

I was taken to the police station and put in a dirty, smelly cell which reminded me unpleasantly of a time when I was a 'lorry girl' in Kent and had been picked up by the police. One of them had looked through the hatch of the cell and called me a sewer rat. It was an unnecessary insult for a young girl. At least, this time, I was wiser, wealthier and able to be bailed out on my own recognisance. The vicar, MP, peer and I often looked back and laughed at what happened. The maid got the sack, she was gutless. Two weeks later in court, the judge said a third conviction would put me in prison for more than an overnight stay. I was heavily fined. (Just another way of paying tax, they said.) I didn't want to close the brothel, so when a bent detective from another squad approached me with a deal, I accepted.

The plan was that if I paid him £100 a week, plus the opportunity to screw me or the girls whenever he fancied it, he'd make sure I didn't get nicked. With this kind of protection I could employ ten girls, each able to service an average of ten clients a day in the 'workrooms', with overspills in my private quarters. This would work out at 100 clients a day on an average fee of £50. Even with deductions for the minder's fee, 50 per cent to the girls (plus paying them extra for servicing the bent tec), and sundry expenses, I could still see a vast weekly profit.

The deal with the tame copper worked well for a year, then he doubled his demand to £200 a week and started showing off to his mates. They'd arrive in a police van, do a sightseeing tour, then expect to have an orgy. I soon got fed up with this and voiced my dissatisfaction.

'C'mon, Lindi, you can spare a few extra fucks for the lads.'

I threw him out with his crew.

I decided keeping a brothel would have to cease. I knew there was a better, probably even more lucrative way I could run my house in Eardley Crescent, and do so alone. But before I got very far with my plans, I was nicked again. I was busted for brothel-keeping when there wasn't another whore in sight!

I was naked on the bed, a client on top, when about half a dozen police burst into the room and stood around us. They pulled him up – 'Off you go, mate' – and then they nicked me. I was totally humiliated, then livid at being fitted up. By now I'd laid off the prostitutes and was working on my own. That certainly wasn't a brothel, but I said nothing, remembering Jake. One of his tips had been: 'Never confirm or deny anything.'

I was innocent of this charge. The police were not required to produce the other whores who were supposedly working at my house or even identify them because our unjust legal system accepts the word of a policeman over that of what is termed a 'common prostitute'. My fictitious helpers were classified Miss A, B and C. They didn't exist!

My solicitor, one of the top men, advised that even though I suspected the police were lying, I had to challenge them on proper grounds. 'There's more than one way to skin a bent cop. We shall play them at their own game.'

He hired a top barrister who he hoped would be mesmerised by my huge tits and be even more determined to win. The barrister set up a plan to confuse the police evidence by drawing different implications from their facts, which would illustrate they were incorrect in their assumptions. He was aided by the solicitor who had obtained the police 'advance evidence'.

In court, under oath, one policeman said: 'I posed as a client and when I knocked at the door, it was answered by a woman [my maid] wearing a red fluffy dressing-gown.' To them, this was a state of undress and proved she was 'doing' clients. But I was one step ahead. I produced my red mohair coat, explaining that my maid had worn it to go out and buy a fresh supply of condoms at the very same time they knocked. This immediately shed doubt on the police evidence.

They then insisted they had seen Miss A, B and C arriving at my premises and not leave for several hours, during which time ninety-three clients were seen entering my house. This, they felt, proved I could not have serviced them all alone. I produced three witnesses to give evidence on my behalf – my maid, an 80-year-old transvestite who was there dressed as a woman, and a builder who had seen what happened. I added that out of the ninety-three men, half were 'bilkers' while many of the others had arrived to make appointments. This again demonstrated that there was an alternative to what the police saw as evidence. It went on in that vein.

When I was in the dock, I wore, on my solicitor's instruction, a cotton shift-dress minus underwear so that my nipples protruded through the flimsy material. I stood up straight, shoulders back, and pushed out my breasts, in order (I hoped) to encourage my barrister. He gave a splendid performance in court! I like to think that my provocative appearance had done the trick.

'Lindi St Clair is a high-profile prostitute. She has two brothel-keeping convictions, to which she pleaded guilty and accepted punishment. She studies law as a hobby and is particularly careful not to break it in her quest to operate an honest, successful and "legal" business. . . .'

He went on to suggest that while the 'good, hard-working' police officers had done an excellent job in stamping out crime, in this case it was regrettable they had misconstrued certain facts – a simple mistake anyone could have made. The case was dismissed, but I was not awarded my costs.

Outside the court, the police were laughing at what had happened, and some of them even invited me for a drink. Since then, I haven't been busted in thirteen years. The Vice Squad seem to be picking on 'green' prostitutes instead, who will plead guilty and not give them a difficult time.

6

The House of Fetish and Fantasy

My brothel had earned me a substantial income. The girls had happily paid me 50 per cent of their earnings, for which I provided safe premises, minders, laundry, heating, electricity, equipment, sex education, health advice, clients and condoms. However, I refused to be pressurised by any more bent cops, and the risk of being busted a third time forced me to examine alternative ways of earning enough cash to keep me in the manner to which I'd become accustomed.

Kinky customers had become a growing part of my clientele at the brothel. They didn't need whores to get their thrills, only someone enterprising like me to set up what they required. The five fetish chambers already in existence had always been kept busy. As Flora used to say, 'one in, one out, keep the pot boiling' – and I did. Now I proposed to expand to ten. I was determined to cater for every fetish and fantasy, and run the best house in town.

Because those clients with sexual quirks enjoyed being left alone to indulge themselves in 'special theme rooms', it was possible for me to work alone as a 'Fetish and Fantasy Mistress', and earn as much cash. It was also completely within the law, although cops with persecution complexes have been known to bust a 'Mistress' working alone, under the 'Disorderly Houses Act'. (Any building in which there is behaviour open to interpretation can be called a disorderly house, even a pub!) I could take in multiple clients, put them in separate rooms, and service them all myself – just like a hairdresser dashes from client to client doing a comb-out, a bleach, a trim, a blow-dry etc, so I could pop from room to room and keep my kinky men satisfied. What made this so ideal was the fact that customers tied up in bondage were hardly able to become impatient and leave. And if they were gagged they could hardly complain!

About 80 per cent of my clients wanted to indulge in some form of 'fetish' or 'fantasy'. I filled a hole in the market because those with a fetish found it difficult, if not impossible, to achieve orgasm without particular props or scenarios incorporated in their service. Men wanting a fantasy liked to be in kinky 'theme rooms' and 'pretend': for example they would *talk* about certain props or scenarios, although in reality they wouldn't be interested in *doing* such things at all.

It may be instructive to describe some of the deviations involved. A 'rubberist' needs to look at, touch, smell or be clad in rubberised material like latex, PVC or vinyl; extremists go for black dustbin sacks, cling film and sticky tape. 'Leatherists' require to look at, touch, smell, wear or be restrained in soft kid or strong hide. Black is the preferred colour because it looks the most deviant. 'Babyists' need mummy Lindi to dress them in nappies, bibs, bonnets and booties, to powder their bottoms and breast-feed them. 'Uniformists' desire to wear or be serviced by someone wearing uniform – military, medical, police, traffic warden, or any other persuasion. Most popular are schoolgirl's and French maid's. 'Shoe lovers' want to worship or wear stiletto heels, the higher and spikier the more exciting. 'Watersport' fetishists desire to be urinated over, some even drink it. (Discreet code words for this in the trade are 'niagara' and 'golden rain'.)

'Domination' is for subservient men who yearn for 'female superiority'. I order them around with dialogue like: 'You are my plaything. You were put on this earth purely to please me. Do you understand? Do my bidding! Madam is waiting!' Humiliation is one step further along the kinky scale. Men are abused and ridiculed. For example I'd mock the size of their penis (even if it were huge), and I'd demand they do horrible things. When they obeyed they felt thoroughly demeaned, but simultaneously aroused. 'Degradation' is the most extreme form of sexual deviation. Depraved perverts (you'd be surprised how many there are) 'need' to experience utter filth like putting their heads down dirty lavatory bowls, and they lust over used condoms and sanitary towels. Personally I find these clients quite revolting.

'TV' is the term used for transvestites, men who like to wear female underwear, dresses, wigs and high heels. Fully-fledged TVs want to wear make-up, false nails, eyelashes and costume jewellery as well.

'Correction' or CP (short for corporal punishment) are the code words for spanking, whipping and caning. Verbal chastisement accompanies this. 'Bondage' incorporates any form of restriction: for example, being secured to a rack, put in a pillory, trussed up like a chicken with ropes, or immobilised with chains and padlocks, leather straps and custom-made restrictive garments like leather straitjackets or inflatable rubber body-bags.

Sado-masochists (S&M) enjoy pain. Just like you or I might enjoy the sensation of being 'tickled', they want to be 'tortured', and fantasise about the death penalty, Colditz and Auschwitz. Some want mild electric shocks on their genitalia, extremists want their nipples, testicles and foreskins pierced. (Since AIDS, many whores have refused to administer S&M services which draw blood. I feel the same.)

'Slaves' are men who place themselves entirely at the Mistress's disposal. 'Domestic' slaves want to be drudges and set to work cleaning, shopping, ironing, etc. 'Sex' slaves want to indulge in 'body worship' (pleasuring women orally or by hand without any sexual gratification for themselves). 'S&M' slaves seek a mixture of domination, bondage, correction, humiliation, degradation and torture – anything goes! Most slaves have split personalities, appearing perfectly 'normal' to their work colleagues, wives and girlfriends, yet secretly they are subservient. Slaves need to 'belong' to a strict woman, and the more assertive she is the better.

To start to fulfil all this, I needed once again to renovate the house at Eardley Crescent. I had to change the floor plan, but fortunately I held the freehold and could therefore do anything I pleased. I had already put in extra doors to allow for discreet entrances and emergency exits. (The entrance favoured by VIP clients was a flat I had rented further along the crescent. From there they could creep over the roof tops into No. 58.) To keep the business going – and the money coming in – chambers six to ten of my House of Fetish and Fantasy were developed one at a time, so that there was always space for clients. I made a positive out of the negative of the builders' commotion, exciting clients by telling them that 'I'm having a new underground torture chamber made *just for you*.'

One early mistake I made was a 'do-it-yourself' torture chamber.

I bought chrome curtain pulleys for a vertical bondage rack. The first punter I tried it on was left up in the air, and the cord – made of a silky twine not designed for body weight – broke. It was not only embarrassing, but the client complained and demanded his £50 back.

To avoid such a disaster ever recurring, I turned to a carpenter I had employed via a kinky magazine ad. He was building me custom-made stocks and pillories, and advised that I get the makings of my vertical bondage rack at a shipyard. I bought a block and tackle and chains that would hold ten tons. This equipment was riveted to the ceiling joists, and no-one ever fell off again!

These were just the beginnings of the House of Fetish and Fantasy. For leather enthusiasts, I laid on supplies from a shop called Atom Age which used to be in Dryden Street, off Drury Lane. I had bondage mittens, the object of which was to totally immobilise the person's hands so they couldn't wiggle their fingers, undo the buckles and escape. Arm gloves served a similar purpose: clients' arms were laced behind their backs from wrist to elbow. Leg cuffs were sheepskin-lined for comfort. A penis corset achieved the opposite: this was a miniature corset complete with laces which were tightened round the shaft of the cock – the bigger the erection, the tighter the corset became. A strap with a heavy weight dangling from the testicles was available as an added attraction. This would add to the 'pleasure'.

I also did very well at a Harrods sale. I saw a saddle on display marked down from £400 to £50. That was too good a bargain to miss, and I made sure I was first in the queue. I would later have an American maid over on a 'working holiday' who delighted in keeping that saddle and all my other leather bondage gear immaculate with saddle soap.

One of my clients recommended that I go to a gunsmith in the Haymarket for handcuffs – a very necessary requisite for those desiring bondage. No-one questioned the fact I wanted fifteen pairs. As they are more generally used for poachers, the salesman probably thought I was a gamekeeper's daughter out shopping (or guessed otherwise, and preferred not to ask)!

I toured stately homes, castles and museums for ideas, and memorised details of potentially useful torture equipment. A scold's bridle, used as a punishment for women in medieval times, was adapted for men with the help of a kinky client who worked in a foundry. A metal piece went over the tongue so that they couldn't talk. It was adjustable to the size of mouth, so wasn't dangerous, and they could still breathe through the nose. It was a great success.

I found different ideas at Edinburgh, Leeds and Warwick castles, but rate Warwick the best when it comes to torture devices. It was there that I got the idea of an *oubliette*. This was a deep, narrow, vertical shaft built into a dungeon floor, covered with a heavy iron grid, where prisoners were left to rot. I could adapt the sewer in my rear yard to fit the same purpose. The manhole cover was prised up, and punters who wanted to suffer humiliation and degradation were pushed down. My mind has always been inventive, and my study of medieval history and language proved useful too – they were sent down accompanied by the appropriate scenario, threats and curses. My *oubliette* was outrageously deviant, and the mere thought that they could be there 'for ever' excited the clients even more.

While researching real dungeons and torture chambers, I would place my hand on the stone walls, close my eyes and 'float back' to medieval times, imagining how it must have been. In this way I was inspired to devise a rotating rack and torture wheel which were then made by my pet carpenter. Once the client was strapped on, he revelled in the dialogue I threw at him as I watched.

'You worthless bastard – look at you – call yourself a man? How dare you come to me with pleas for mercy!'

The insults could be tailored to the person or their profession. For instance, an accountant was 'tested'.

'What's one and one?'

'Two.'

'No, it's eleven, you incompetent!' I would then slap and lash him.

All the torture chambers had mirrored walls. The fact that clients could see their reflection magnified their pleasure.

Suffering was the prime motive of clients coming to the House of Fetish and Fantasy. Some would be specific with their requests, and there was no end to the degradation they wanted to experience. In trying to fulfil all their wishes, I called the film man I had met a few years back on the plane from Paris. Up until then we had kept in touch with the occasional phone call and yearly Christmas card. Now I wondered if there were anything from horror films which would fit in with what I needed or which might be copied.

We met for lunch out at the studios, after which I was free to tour the store of props and take my pick of stuff to be delivered to Earl's Court. I spotted an iron maiden which I thought would be perfect. It reminded me of those wooden Russian dolls with smaller and smaller ones inside. A real iron maiden is a six-foot, man-shaped iron case lined with iron spikes. The ones on the door are the longest so that when it is slammed shut on the victim, he suffers an agonisingly slow death from multiple stab wounds. The iron maiden I found was only a fake with rubber spikes, but it created a horrific optical illusion.

One of my clients wanted something 'spiky' on a smaller scale. For him, I made a special thin black leather strap which had drawing pins pushed through it. This was slipped round his penis (spikes facing inwards) and the bigger his erection grew, the deeper the pins pricked him. Masochists found this a most 'exquisite and delicious pain'.

Rubber was an important element of many fetishes. I had my 'rubber room' lined with rolls of latex bought from Weathervane. For way-out rubber restriction, I had a special inflatable cocoon made from two layers of latex. Air was pumped into it from an oxygen cylinder, and the suit blew up to something resembling a Michelin man. This pressure of air between the latex layers forced the inner rubber lining to tighten around the body. In this type of bondage, the client couldn't see, hear or smell, and could only breathe through a little mouth tube that had air valves.

Some liked me to warn them, 'I'm going to turn off your air, you odious article.'

In my early days, an economist used to like me to say: 'You love the pressure of inflation, don't you?'

The variations on this particular rubber suit included inflating the hood and gag to create a sensation of smothering, and the latex round the penis to cause a tight grip which was like masturbation.

As the brothel was gradually transformed into a unique series of fetish and fantasy chambers, some of the house's original features were adapted. A large Victorian brick fireplace became a 'cell' complete with iron bars. For extra humiliation, slaves were made to stand on tiptoe with their heads up the chimney. In the old scullery I installed a king-size jacuzzi bath where several couples could frolic. This eventually became my 'cannibal room', inspired by a visit to Rio de Janeiro. There I witnessed a kind of voodoo ceremony (or *macumba* as they call it), when a circle of women chanting round a young man transformed him into an old Chinaman who uttered strange sounds.

I couldn't quite accomplish that, but I reproduced the Brazilian jungle in the bathroom with giant rubber plants and a profusion of hanging vines. I played the Cannibal Queen – more an Amazon warrior really, with loin cloth and sharp spear – pushing the client down into the jacuzzi 'cooking pot', to boil with carrots, onions and Oxo cubes.

I stood guard: 'I'm going to cook you, then eat you.'

The jacuzzi bubbled. I poked the victim with my spear. 'Let's see if you are done.'

Insults were tossed in for flavour. I'd lift out the pink penis which had shrivelled in the water. 'Useless! Worthless!'

Humiliation was what it was all about.

I fitted one of the dungeons with a gallows where clients were 'hanged'. You had to be very careful with this game. They wanted a rope round their neck, and you had to pull it just so tight to keep the illusion going. One man got too excited. His hands and feet were also tied, and when he lunged forward on the shout of 'Hang the prisoner!', he almost strangled. It was hard to get him down because he was covered in a rubber cat suit which was slippery with perspiration. It didn't help that he weighed about fourteen stone. I did finally manage to get the rope off, but I was a bit frantic because he'd passed out. It only lasted a few seconds, and when he came round, he didn't know what had happened.

I had one other scare when I'd strapped a man on to a rack. I left him while I went to fetch the vibrator from another room, and got an electric shock from accidentally touching a bare wire (left after extending the lead to facilitate clients furthest from the plug socket). Had I been electrocuted, my strapped-down client would also have died because no-one knew he was down in the dungeon. I realised that when the business was fully operational, I would need someone else on hand. I couldn't be entirely alone.

After a series of temporary maids, I put out the word on the prostitutes' grapevine that I wanted a reliable maid who could be discreet. Shelley knocked on my door one morning and was asked in for tea and a chat. I immediately warmed to her. Not only was she a 'Mumsy' sort of person, but her husband happened to be a gangster. This reminded me of my relationship with Jake. I felt comfortable with this underworld connection, and knew she wouldn't quake at the knees if the police came calling again.

For, as I said, even though I was no longer running a brothel, I was never quite sure when an over-zealous cop would nick me for a 'disorderly house'. As I was now extremely busy – my reputation for producing 'surprises' was spreading – the number of visitors to the house increased. This could well start a ripple of interest from the Vice Squad, and we had to be prepared. I knew Shelley would be able to cope.

In fact, with Shelley on hand to receive clients, the intake increased even more. Some shy ones came to the door with notes explaining what they wanted: 'Dear Miss St Clair, I've sent Johnnie to you because I caught him looking up my skirt.' They would then come in and quietly wait until I devised the appropriate punishment, and the costume to go with it. A 'smacked bottie' was simple, as I had a choice of bare hands, paddles and pinpong bats. So was being 'Nanny', because I had an over-sized cradle in which to rock 'baby' to sleep, and then 'Mummy' would give them a bottle or change king-sized nappies. A dentist was more explicit. He wanted to wear a bride's dress and be tied to pretend railroad tracks like a silent-movie heroine. A sportsman required me to wear red boxing gloves and punch him on the nose until he bled: this particular weekly service carried a fee of £100.

Possibly the most unusual and easiest request to fulfil came in a letter: 'Dear Mistress, I've got this fantasy, can you help me? I like to be ironed. I like a woman to stand over me with a warm iron and take all my creases out.' He became a regular client for seven years. He'd undress and I'd stand over him wearing a white apron and nothing else. The iron would be just warm enough for him to feel good.

Another fantasy enjoyed by several clients involved being strapped to a crucifix which stood on a platform in one of the dungeons. The platform had a trapdoor in it, and when a lever was pushed, it dropped open, leaving the slave's feet dangling in mid-air. Usually, for this particular scenario, I dressed as a nun, but one of my holidays gave me the idea of how to instil an even greater sense of the bizarre. I'd been on a world tour to look at brothels in other countries and, bored with the tawdriness of what I saw in New Orleans, I'd persuaded a cab-driver to find me something different. We drove out to the border of Louisiana and Mississippi where a brothel known as the Cat House operated in a wood shack on the swamp's edge. (This was much favoured by the Louisiana police force, and in the few days I stayed there, I sold sex to half of them at 20 dollars a 'go'. I'm a sucker for a southern accent!) One of the whores had a pet alligator with only one leg, and used to threaten to feed it with her clients' penises. Since alligators are in short supply in Earl's Court, I settled for telling my clients there were snakes writhing in the trapdoor pit under the crucifix. They loved it!

As so many of my clients were now into bondage and discipline, I developed a way to service several at the same time. With the help of one of my ex-biker friends – he'd originally come to set up the security camera for my front door – I had the dungeons bugged. (He was by now a respected electronics expert who had bugged various embassies. It was rather satisfying to know we had both got on so well in our respective fields.) And a punter I called 'Dick the Scientist' advised on the development of what I called a 'de-spunker'. This was an elasticated loop with a vibrator the size of a ten-pence piece attached. The loop went round the shaft of the cock so that the vibrator was on the knob. A fifty-foot wire was attached to the de-spunker with a bell press at the other ends. I could carry a handful of these at a time. While the maid and I played Kaluki, we were able to listen to the punters' groans, and every so often, to add to their suffering, I'd push my buttons and give them a 'buzz'. This became a very popular service.

By now I had developed a series of nicknames for my clients derived from their jobs, sexual deviations or professions. They included 'The Field Marshal' who loved to be beaten; 'Legs Eleven', a transvestite social worker, 'Jasper the Gas-Mask Vicar'; 'Deep Throat' from the Cabinet; the 'Carry-On Kink' (now dead) who sneaked in with his hat pulled down and his collar up so that Hattie Jacques (his fellow *Carry On* star) who lived opposite wouldn't recognise him; and 'Gang Bang', a VIP's son, who pays me £20,000 to be raped by ten women of different races (Indian, African, Icelandic, Brazilian, Chinese, Dutch, Canadian, Swedish, Russian and myself as the 'Cockney').

Another character was 'Bearskin', a Grenadier Guard who broke the rules by sneaking his uniform out from his barracks to wear during a sex session. 'Sunshine', so named because he never smiles, has been coming to me for twenty years. He calls me his 'big, fat white whore', and asks me to say, 'Enjoy my flesh, Master.' He often calls from abroad to book an appointment. I still don't know his name, and when I ask it, he says, 'I come for business, not to be personal.' However, little clues make me suspect he is connected to a royal family.

I have so many clients who loved to be flogged, that a sorely aching shoulder which requires medication – the doctor likens it to tennis elbow – has become an occupational hazard.

Once a request for a whipping enabled me to get my own back on the judiciary in a slightly devious way. I had lost a court case to the tune of £20,000, the judge having found against me. I was discussing this with a regular, 'Judge Bottoms Up', and gave him more than his money's worth when I took out my annoyance on his backside!

My maid began to recognise more and more famous faces as our intake of clients grew. I was more concerned with remembering their cocks. A client would often express surprise if his face wasn't instantly recognised by me, and my standard response was: 'That was over a thousand men ago.' I never forgot a cock, though, whether it was crooked, knobbly, minuscule or oversized, and once I'd seen his, I'd say, 'Oh yes, I do remember you.' I could write a book about the penis! I've seen over 41,460 specimens and administered over 135,350 services over the last twenty years.

It began to be noticeable after a time that a lot of special equipment was being nicked. No matter how much I watched those men, they were managing to steal from under my nose. Canes would go down their sleeves or the legs of their trousers. They'd also steal souvenirs from the parts of the building I kept for private use. Sometimes I looked on it as a compliment because, when I was a young rebel, I used to pinch ashtrays and glasses from pubs as souvenirs. I began to understand how peeved the publicans must have felt. I'd lose panties, bras and stiletto boots, including one very special pair I'd bought from the Let It Rock shop in King's Road, run by Vivienne Westwood and Malcolm Maclaren.

My equipment was more serious, though. Clients may have been tempted to take items because of my claim that the small pieces of torture equipment were specially made in Hamburg, a city with a reputation for sexual extravagance. As it happens, all my stuff was British, and very expensive. The leather gag adapted from the scold's bridle cost me £200 in the mid seventies, for instance. It would be at least £600 today.

Most losses had to go down as business expenses, but some things were irreplaceable, such as an antique whip I treasured, used by a Virginian plantation overseer in the days of slavery. (I'm very keen on period exotica, and am now on Sotheby's mailing list. I hope one day to bid for the prototype of today's vibrator.)

Bad behaviour came in all forms. What probably made me the most furious was the professor at a London college who had the nerve to pee in my waste basket before his service began. I threw him out in the street, his clothes after him, and he had to stand there in full view of everyone to get dressed. He was very angry, but so was I at his bad manners. I sent a bill to his college for a £50 'cleaning' fee, and he paid it!

I began to see that if my clients were going to behave badly, or steal my stuff, I'd do better with minders on the premises again for protection. The going rate was 25 per cent of whatever I earned while they were on duty. They stayed out of sight until needed, usually playing cards in whatever room happened to be free. One of them was Charlie, a former bouncer in a nightclub, with whom I had a brief affair. When we parted friends, he became my minder.

To prevent any further nicking of my property – the incon-venience of replacing special items was as irritating as the loss – I installed a security system similar to those in department stores. Every piece of my equipment was tagged with little white plastic security discs which set off alarm bells if the client tried to sneak them past the laser beam by my front door. Caught red-handed, they would be searched by Charlie. My property was removed and they were 'fined'. It was either £50 or he blacked their eyes. I had no compunction about that. I had given them excellent value for money, and they had then had the gall to rob me.

The other problem was with a punter who wanted his money back because he had changed his mind. I told him he was in breach of contract. I'd learned the law of contract and consumer redress in my early twenties when I'd been nicked in a dispute over £5. I had accepted a client for a £5 'quickie'. We lay on the bed, fondled each other, then I unwrapped a condom and tried to put it on him. He refused to wear it, and demanded his money back. First, I tried to explain it was for hygiene reasons, then refused to return the money because he had already had some fondling which cost £5 anyway. He went to the police and accused me of stealing the money. Two bobbies called round and, without allowing me to get dressed, I was carted off in my 'peek-a-boo' bra and cutaway panties.

'Look, love,' said the sergeant in charge. 'He's paid for a fuck and he hasn't had one. He's an awkward bastard so give him back his fiver and we'll forget it.'

Fuming over the freebie fondle, I was forced to return it. (Actually, I later learned that a contract made between a prostitute and client is not enforceable by law, so the police had no right to intervene. This particular incident was out of their jurisdiction.) At least I took the sergeant's advice. I must make clear to every client beforehand that condoms must be worn, so I ordered signs from a local printer:

RULES OF THE HOUSE
1. Condoms must be worn at all times.
2. Clients who change their minds are not entitled to a refund.

These signs were displayed prominently in all the rooms thereafter.

Now, I was faced with a client who obviously hadn't paid attention to the second house rule. He stood his ground in my hall with his coat and briefcase, and said he'd stand there all day to upset the business. It didn't bother the other punters at all. They just went past him because I was saying: 'Don't mind him, he's a slave and gets a kick out of standing in the hall.' He went in the end.

Slaves of all kinds were acceptable to other visitors, and by now I had quite a few of them. They'd appear at the door: 'Can I be your slave, Madam?' I'd ask them how much they had to spend, and on that depended what they did for me. Much was made up as I went along, and if I liked them. I had one who wanted to crouch naked on all fours. The maid and I played Kaluki on his back. Good-looking slaves got my services at a discount, as did the useful ones like gardeners, plumbers and bricklayers, some of whom had been involved in renovating the house. There were several who have been coming to me for years, in some cases since before they were married. (They only come now if they can sneak off from their wives.)

One elderly gentleman of seventy does the best domestic work I have ever seen. Another slave tried to get rid of him, and they would bicker over who would wash up, peel the potatoes, or sweep the floor. I managed to smooth over their quarrel.

The masochistic slaves are all rechristened 'Dennis' after the man who murdered the Countess. It is my way of avenging her death, and they are the ones who get the 'bonus' of a free, merciless beating down in my dungeons. In any case it is part of the game they need to play to achieve orgasm, no matter how much they protest. On one occasion, I took pity on a man who started to cry. He even offered me money to release him. 'Please stop, I've made a mistake, let me go.' I believed him and did so. After all, he *was* the client. The next day, a letter came through the door: 'Dear Madam, you let me go. I was very disappointed. You are not a very good Mistress. I am not coming back.'

That was a lesson well learned. From then on, however much they scream to be released, I ignore them. I just turn up the music and drown them out. I know, as their Mistress, they have given me the right to decide when they can be freed. Dedicated 'Dennises' even went so far as to draw up 'Bonds of Servitude', documents binding them to devotion and obedience. They wanted to be my chattel, for me to 'own' them. One particular man who worked at Buckingham Palace went a step further. He deliberately posed for scandalous photographs and instructed me to send them to the *News of the World* if ever he displeased me.

Some slaves required other forms of servitude or domination for their enjoyment. I have an MP who, like other recognisable people, always comes in via the back door. He calls me by his teacher's name. She used to cane him and he likes to relive the experience. The maid sends him to 'teacher's study' at the top of the stairs. I am there, in a mortar board and gown, and working up a rage.

'Come in, Flatfoot Junior.' This is the name he has chosen for himself. I cane his hands, the backs of his legs, then pull down his trousers, and bend him over the desk for six of the best. He is scolded for his sloppy writing and for having ink blots on his notebook, then has to practise neat handwriting by doing 'lines'. How he accomplishes this varies. Once I made him get out his cheque book and write 'Pay Miss St Clair £50' on each remaining cheque. He happily did so, and usually he paid me £600 plus per session!

Another MP was one of the many closet bisexuals in Parliament who used to go 'cottaging' (picking up men in public lavatories). The in-joke among us whores was that Parliament needed a Division Bell (the bell that summons MPs to vote) in all of the public toilets in the borough of Westminster! I had a special 'cock-stool' made to accommodate his needs. He sat on this, positioning his anus over a hole 2 inches in diameter. His penis was strapped on to a little pedestal and his wrists and ankles secured to the stool's four legs. A lever when operated pushed a dildo through the hole for anal intercourse. (He knew the law backwards, and told me that anal sex between a consenting man and woman is illegal, and carries a sentence of life imprisonment! Not many people know that!)

Some of the requests I found really odd – such as the 'Rear Admiral' who likes to be shot. He falls down, I say 'You're dead!', and push the gun even more deeply into his body: 'You're very dead, you're the deadest person ever.' I still have a cupboard full of the air guns and starting pistols he brought for this service. He is probably equalled by 'Flicker', the rock vocalist who likes hot candle wax dripping on his erection. For him I say: 'I've got an "extra-hot" flame today, hotter than usual.' And he believes it!

A more light-hearted request came from a tennis player whose fetish is wearing frilly pantaloons and a frilly maid's outfit. He used to want to be called the Parlour Room Knicker Maid, and would come to work as a slave in this costume whenever I was entertaining.

There were also couples who wanted my assistance in their games. An army major and his wife needed to be tied up facing each other, then to watch as I gave them individual vibro 'treatment'. A tycoon from the Channel Isles arrives with a different secretary each time. They dress in rubber and have sex in the rubber room while I take photographs.

Lesbian clients are less in number. There's an heiress who wants to be stretched on the rack and dildo'd by a tyrannical lesbian dictator, and a gynaecologist who fantasises about being caned by a prostitute. (She keeps me supplied with latex surgeon's gloves and syringes for my medical services.)

I used to receive clients in the office before they went off to partake of their fantasies. The maid would also give them a cup of tea there afterwards, when they had reverted to their public persona. There was never any embarassment, once I had learned not to refer to what had just happened. It was a service, but not one to be discussed once provided.

In lieu of cash, I sometimes accepted goods or professional advice. There was the Harrods fish delivery man who came round weekly on his bicycle and left a side of smoked salmon afterwards; a man who worked at Burberrys who bartered a £60 service for a £250 raincoat. I still think the funniest was the man who paid me in two large cartons of Whiskas. Forty-eight tins at a time kept my cats very happy!

I'm still often asked if I'll take goods instead of money – and why not? After all, by then I'd begun to count clients in terms of what they'd get for me. In a busy week, I could see two hundred men through the doors of the House of Fetish and Fantasy. Forty men meant a mink, and I soon had several. A hundred meant a car, though it took a lot more than that to get a Jaguar XJ6, then a Mercedes, and later a Rolls Corniche convertible and a personalised licence plate. No matter, I was enjoying life!

7

Friends and Enemies

The business and the transformation of the brothel into the House of Fetish and Fantasy were beginning to crowd me out of my living quarters in Eardley Crescent, so I needed to have a home separate from it all. I wasn't short of money, it was piling in and begging to be spent. I was never one for having a lot of clothes (in my business I am rarely fully dressed!), so I bought only a few classic items once a year; I didn't really drink except socially; never smoked and never took drugs. My greatest indulgence was food, which would eventually spoil my figure. So I had quite a lot of money saved.

I was able therefore to indulge in one of my hobbies, looking at and, on occasion, buying property. I felt like a businesswoman playing Monopoly for real. Now I had an eye out for a house for my own use. One or two had appealed, but nothing had attracted me until I was stuck in a traffic jam outside an estate agent long enough to read the details in the window. I was drawn to a property on the Goldsmith Estate in East Acton. It was a big house with a large garden, where I planned to install a swimming pool as soon as I could. The cost was £39,000, quite a lot of money in 1979.

Everything about it seemed right, even the extent of street access from the back. (Although I envisaged this as a place for my private pleasure, one never knew when a quick exit might be appropriate.) I designed the interior myself. I wanted an ultra modern theme – all very James Bond. Upstairs had custom-built rust suede furniture, cream shag-pile carpets and peach mirrored walls. The beds revolved and cocktail bars, TV, stereos and flashing disco lights were built into the headboards. Looking back, I now shudder at my over-the-top taste – a total contrast to the elegant Louis XIV decor I had had at Earl's Court. I also designed the garden in yellow, pink and white. I planted so many flowers, shrubs and trees that I had to dig up half the lawn to accommodate them. I was Syon Park's best customer for a while. I moved in when Eardley Crescent was undergoing renovations, and travelled to work every day.

Although my House of Fetish and Fantasy took up a lot of time, it didn't prevent me from having some social life. I had boyfriends, and those that knew who I was accepted that my business was separate from personal pleasure, just as Jake had done for a while; others not in the know were 'ordinary' boyfriends, just like anyone else would have. I lived two quite different lives.

The first man who asked me to marry him was a Grenadier Guard. Guards are not allowed to speak on duty, so when he was at Buckingham Palace, I'd go down there and talk to him through the railings, deliberately trying to distract him. When he was in a sentry-box outside St James's Palace, I used to talk dirty to him and watch his trousers swell. Sadly, before we had a chance to make many plans, he was sent to Northern Ireland where he was blown up and killed while on patrol.

There were some boyfriend-minders like Charlie, heavies who kept a professional eye on me. If we fancied each other we would have an affair, but that would have nothing to do with money. I met men in various other ways too – when I was abroad or in discos or pubs, and on one occasion because one of my maids bragged about working for Lindi St Clair. A friend of hers said he'd like to go out with me, and she fixed us a date.

I had one boyfriend who was a policeman. He originally came knocking at my door investigating a murder. We clicked, he returned for more questions, we went out for a drink, then started dating. I like going with police officers, as it makes me feel lawful, and what a man does is bound to have an effect on a woman. This was a straight sex scene, and our friendship has continued. He has proved that not every policeman is out to get me for what I do. He certainly knew of my profession from the start.

Sometimes, when I met a new man, I used a different name because, by the late seventies, Lindi St Clair was well-known for what she did. I took boyfriends back to the other flat, further down Eardley Crescent, and on one occasion, as we went past 58, one boyfriend sneered: 'That's where that tart Lindi St Clair lives.' Silly bastard, didn't realise he was out with her! I often hear of straight people who had never met me bragging that they had. It's amazing how people jump on the bandwagon.

I also had a number of friends (and 'enemies') in my own world, amongst the local prostitutes and fantasy mistresses.

There are three levels of prostitution, and each geographical area contains close-knit cliques. The 'top' level comprises hard-core older girls who have chosen prostitution as their vocation, and have successfully built up established businesses. The 'middle' level comprises semi-professionals and part-time amateurs who whore to amass capital for setting up straight businesses like boutiques or restaurants. The 'bottom' level are girls soliciting on the streets as a means of survival. And with the exception of new girls working their way up the prostitution ladder, street whores are either under-age runaways or no-hopers without incentive who would remain at the bottom of any job. I've mingled with them all.

From the early seventies, the Earl's Court 'middle' clique consisted of sixty to seventy girls aged between eighteen and thirty, some older, who rented bent flats in the multi-tenanted large Victorian houses near the tube and the Exhibition Hall. Their population (which the authorities have always under-estimated) fluctuated as they were exposed, got nicked, diseased, pregnant, bashed up or murdered. As one girl went, another replaced her from hundreds waiting on a local estate-agent's list.

Members of the 'top' clique, with whom I socialised at weekends, were Kate, Nancy and Lola. Mistress Kate worked from a basement flat in a street near me. She was six feet tall, slim, forty, with long black hair; she wore tight black leather catsuits. When she wasn't working she lived in a mansion furnished with Chinese antiques and she drove a Range Rover with two jewel-collared dogs sitting proudly in the back. She had an elderly slave whom she'd make run along behind her car as she drove down Earl's Court Road. She specialised in 'transvestite maid training'.

Mistress Lola was a well-groomed, fifty-year-old transsexual. She was a millionairess with a luxury home in West London and a basement work flat five streets away from me. She specialised in what she called 'quick volume', whereby she let clients do absolutely anything at all for a set fee of £20. Her earnings were phenomenal and her motto was 'It's better to let fifty "tiddlers" turn you inside out than wait all day for a "biggy".' She only worked three days a week, and spent the rest of her time putting massage cards in shop windows and showing off in her flashy convertible.

Mistress Nancy was seventy-five. She'd spent £20,000 on cosmetic surgery and didn't look a day over fifty-five. She owned a lavish home just outside London and a house near me where she kept a live-in slave. I met Archie, a retired trades unionist, after he'd followed me home from the shops. It was raining and my wellingtons and PVC cape turned him on. From then on he moonlighted behind Nancy's back and crept round to my house to cook cheese omelettes (my favourite food then) and empty my dustbins. It felt funny, having a slave 'two-timing' his Mistress. Nancy specialised in 'colonic irrigation'. She had been on the game for fifty years and had retained all her clients. Some had been nobodies years before, but now many had prospered and become big-time household names. 'They've grown old with me, ducky, and they feel safe. There are too many kiss-and-tell opportunists around.'

I used to wonder if I'd still be on the game at Nancy's age, shuddering at the thought of ending up a bag lady, or like another local whore called Sheena. She was fifty, a drunken has-been, who worked in hair rollers and down-at-heel slippers. Her regulars were lonely old drunks whom she got more drunk with.

Around this time, when the Yorkshire Ripper was at large, I only accepted 'Regulars' and 'Been Befores', turning 'Strangers' away. These latter were simply 'passing trade', men who responded to massage adverts on the spur of the moment. They were always secretive about their identities, and funnily enough, the more secretive they were, the lower down the social ladder they were (like odd-job men, factory workers and dustmen).

On quiet days, to amuse myself, I would visit my friend 'Charlotte the Harlot', whom I'd first met when a client brought her along for a lesbian scene at my West Kensington flat. She belonged to the Knightsbridge 'top' clique, and lived near Harrods. The Ripper scare cost me lots of business, so when no regulars were booked in I'd 'work' Harrods with her. She was forever lurking in top stores and easily recognised regular affluent shoppers. We'd pick them up in the Food Hall and take them across the road to her flat.

Occasionally I'd get involved on the fringes of the 'bottom' levels. From the late seventies, lack of opportunity had brought thousands of amateur prostitutes from the Midlands and the North flooding into the West End, taking flats in Paddington, Euston and King's Cross. These girls were troublesome and exceedingly jealous of anyone who made more money than them. They frequently beat up their rivals, sabotaged their adverts, and cut their telephone wires.

A hierarchy developed. The toughest, most devious girl became 'Queen' and dictated to the others. One particularly nasty 'Queen' was a good-looking, buxom forty-five-year-old from Birmingham with a history of drugs and violence. She had a Jamaican pimp, eight children who were in care, and she'd been in prison for attempted murder. Occasionally I socialised with her at a West End drinking club, which just so happened to be a popular haunt of off-duty police officers. I couldn't believe it when I heard gossip that a corrupt cop wanted to trade cocaine for sex. Rumour had it that he creamed off cocaine for himself before handing in booty from drug raids. 'Queen' had a steamy affair with him: they'd sniff coke and screw all afternoon, and he became besotted with her. 'I can twist him round my little finger,' she'd boast. And to prove it she persuaded him to 'fit up' her rivals, leaving the area clear for her to work without competition. Whenever anyone pulled her up over this, she got her 'tame cop' to give them an ultimatum. 'Pack up and move on, otherwise you'll be nicked.' Nobody argued with him, and nobody dared report him to Scotland Yard – the repercussions could be too great.

The Earl's Court 'top' clique used to socialise at an unlicensed late-night restaurant in Westbourne Grove which sold alcohol in china teapots. I didn't enjoy drinking white wine from teacups, so I usually opted for the company of the Earl's Court 'middle' clique, who were mostly lesbians. They hung out at the Gateways Club off King's Road, Louise's Club off Oxford Street, and various other gay clubs.

I've never had any problem with gay people. When I was on the street we had congregated in the cafés after working hours. The gays in the clubs were intrigued by me. Before I saw the sense of the anti-fur lobby, I was a mink-coated, flamboyant character freely offering champagne. And over the years, coming up the ladder in the prostitution game, I'd met, then later employed, lesbians. They make the best whores. It's a living for them and has nothing to do with their personal lives. They detest men and can therefore switch off and be screwed all day without a care. Men don't register in their emotions. Having lesbians for the brothel had made good sense too. Heterosexual or nymphomaniac whores can be a problem because they sometimes fancy their clients and get annoyed if they lose the horn. It's worse when they fall in love and run off with them – you lose both a good worker *and* a good customer!

Even the lesbian scene had its hierarchy, and at that time the top girls were four flashy lesbians, Agnes, Chris, Biff and Val. I had lots of lesbian friends, but I was fascinated by Agnes from the moment I saw her. She had charisma, yet at the same time she was creepy. There was a rumour that she'd chopped up her mother's pet poodles with an axe because she was jealous of them. Who knows if it was true! Agnes and her mother were both Earl's Court whores. Chris was a whore too, working in South Kensington, but Biff and Val were clip girls.

I'd heard about clip girls when I was a stripper in the late sixties, but I never really knew how they operated. Biff demonstrated it to me. She solicited what she called 'mug punters', and tempted them with ridiculously cheap offers at a fraction of the market price. 'Hello, darling, you can have anything you like, come as often as you like, for only £10.' The true price for such a service was more like £50, so the 'bargain' was too good to refuse. To convince them further she'd say, 'Because you're not a regular, you need to pay a deposit in case you break anything in the room.' This seemed reasonable, and punters happily handed over £100, sometimes even more. 'Don't worry, I'll give you a receipt. The deposit is kept in the Madam's safe, and you'll get it back afterwards.' Their receipts made them feel secure. Then Biff would say, 'I can't walk with you in case the police are watching, so meet me up the road at . . . .' She'd give a fake address and disappear with the cash.

Sometimes, she said, the same punters were clipped repeatedly. I was amazed that grown men were so stupid!

'Personally, I would prefer to do the sex, it's less hassle,' I said.

'Uugghh! Not likely. I'm not going to be used as a spunk disposal unit for men,' was her answer to this. Biff was a thirty-year-old virgin who despised men to such a degree that she thought they should all be rounded up and exterminated!

Biff's girlfriend was Tracy (a whore who worked around the corner from me); Agnes and Chris were a long-standing couple, so it seemed convenient for me to pair off with Val. I wasn't bisexual, I was trisexual (I'll try anything once), and I invited Val to move into the Acton house. I was always the feminine, passive partner in a lesbian affair. In some ways, it was no different from sex with a man. You are lying there taking it. I could never be butch, I felt silly. The advantage of lesbian sex is that there is no smelly semen, or risk of pregnancy or disease; and unlike a real prick, the dildo stays hard forever! The trouble with a lesbian relationship is that although there is a lot of love and affection, there is also a lot of jealousy. This was to prove very damaging for me.

Val was a red-haired butch who liked to have money spent on her. I willingly complied, constantly giving her cash, until one day I saw her at the club buying champagne for an old girlfriend. She also grew jealous of my favourite slave. I'd grown very fond of him over the years, and his fetish was simple – wearing purple crutchless knickers whilst fetching and carrying for a dominant woman. He was a BR train driver, on the London to Penzance route, and confessed to wanking over porno mags in his cab whilst the train sped along on automatic. Occasionally he was given time off to study signal boxes along the track, but he visited me instead.

Val made me choose between them, so I had to let him go, a decision I've regretted ever since. She was hot-tempered and she gave me black eyes. I was mentally stronger, but she was physically stronger than me and my only retaliation was to hire a thug to bash her. Unfortunately this backfired because it made her even more angry. The last straw was after we'd been to Ascot. I'd spent forever finding a fancy hat for Ladies Day, and as we waited for the train home, Val pushed me off the platform. I managed to scramble back but my hat fell off on to the rails. Before I had a chance to pick it up, the train came along and ran it over.

I phoned Chris for a sympathetic ear, but she'd just split up with Agnes and sought comfort herself. She came round with two bottles of red wine and we drowned our sorrows together. She was into the *ouija* board, so I made one by placing the bathroom mirror on the floor and arranging plastic Scrabble letters around the edge. I placed an upturned glass in the centre and we positioned our fingers gently on the top.

They say that when you're at a low ebb, tired or distressed, your spiritual guard is down and you're susceptible to bad spirits. So before we began, Chris said a prayer to protect us from evil. 'Is anybody there? My name is Chris, will you speak to me?' This was repeated for about 10 minutes, then the glass slowly glided across the mirror, stopping at various letters to spell out the name 'Seth'. 'Who are you?' Chris asked. 'A disciple of Jesus,' he replied. I was excited and spooked at the same time; I asked his advice about Val and he warned: 'Beware, they will kill you!' It seemed a bit severe, but clinched my decision to dump her. Then he spelt out dirty words which frightened me. I took my finger off the glass. 'We're going now, will you speak to me again?' asked Chris. 'Yes.' Then she said, 'God bless.' It made her feel safe in case he tried to possess us. She was more experienced with *ouija* than I was and told me to disregard Seth's warning. 'Spirits tell lies sometimes,' she said reassuringly. 'It was probably a mischievous one hanging around on the other side with nothing better to do.'

We spent the night together which led to a short affair before Agnes came back. Val then left for San Francisco (we never heard of her again) and I took off to Australia for a change of scenery. It was August, a bad time to visit Sydney, as it was pouring with rain. I asked a cab driver which paper advertised prostitutes, and bought *The Ribald*. I was pleasantly surprised to find a picture and an article about me. The main brothels were in an area called King's Cross, and a few more discreet ones were located in Surrey Hills. One called the Nevada looked the most lively because it had a dozen whores displaying themselves on the first-floor balcony. They called out to prospective punters below, then went inside, swopped clothes and wigs, and reappeared. This gave the illusion of a wider choice of whores. A clever ruse, I thought, and went inside for a job. A steep flight of stairs took me to the first-floor parlour which incorporated a bar and a jukebox. Madam was snugly installed behind a hatch, as if selling cloakroom tickets. She looked me up and down with suspicion, but relaxed once I introduced myself.

'Can I hang out for a while?' I asked.

'Sure, make yourself at home. The bedrooms are all en-suite on the second floor.' She gave me what must have been her basic instructions to new girls, then apologised when I gave a knowing smile. 'Sorry, it's force of habit. I forgot I was talking to a real pro.'

I worked at the Nevada for a few weeks, but I wasn't very popular with the clients because I insisted on a condom – the others didn't. The split was 70–30 in the girls' favour, but the Madam refused my money. 'That's OK. It's on the house.' One thing there proved to me forever that men are thick. A client turned my natural self down:

'No thanks, you're too fat.' Ten minutes later, I was wearing a black wig and he approached me. 'Oh yes, you're lovely, can we go upstairs?'

I made friends with two flat-chested prostitutes, Kelly and Phoebe, who needed a busty girl to make a foursome for their 'sugar-daddy'. They had an old bus and were driving across the Nullabor Plain to Kalgoorlie to meet him, so I went along for fun. Big Hank was a cropduster, with a fetish for flying naked women in his plane before finishing off in a foursome in his hangar, with drinks and dirty songs. He took us to his home, a remote place which I couldn't pronounce, then flew us around in his four-seater plane which looked like a cross between a glider and an old-fashioned war machine. Kelly and he sat naked in the front, Phoebe and I naked in the back. My enormous tits were pummelled by the g force and the wind ripped my false eyelashes off. It was the most awkward 500 dollars I'd ever earned! The best thing about it was composing dirty lyrics, which came easily to me. (This skill later developed into my forming a band, Whiplash and the Merry Madams, and I sent kinky sex songs to MPs during election campaigns!)

Kelly and Phoebe were both twenty-five. They rejected per-manent homes and opted for travelling around Australia, living and working in various brothels. I accompanied them to a place known as The Shack near Kalgoorlie, which catered especially for miners. It was a ramshackle wooden hut, with sweaty men clad in jeans, vests and wide-brimmed hats, drinking tins of beer and chewing gum. As an English 'Sheila' (woman) I was very welcome, so I decided to spend a few weeks working and sightseeing. It seemed funny having miners for clients after once owning the deeds to one.

Before I left for home, I gleaned the names and addresses of every Australian MP under 70, and the details of Australia's 500 richest men. More potential customers to add to my mail-shot list.

During my vacation, 'Queen's' tame cop apparently used his influence to bust quite a few big earners, and her junkie friends from Sheffield, Leeds and Manchester took over their flats. They had no principles and rifled through their clients' wallets, stealing cash, credit cards and driving licences. Some clients retaliated by later returning to beat them up. But by then the culprits had returned up North and new girls had taken their place. Unfortunately, an irate punter cannot distinguish between one whore and another, and many undeserving girls became victims of their revenge. This triggered off a spate of 'whore-bashing' whereby gangs of thugs waited for clients to depart, then, posing as clients themselves, gained entry, overpowered the girls and let in accomplices waiting outside. The girls were raped, robbed and beaten, sometimes even hospitalised, but they were too scared to call the police. Those who did either met with no response or were told by 'Queen's' tame cop to pack up and leave the area otherwise they would be nicked for running a disorderly house.

The whore-bashers spread further afield, armed with knives and guns. The grapevine buzzed with their descriptions – two white men, one blonde, one dark, both about twenty-five, and a younger black man. As I expected, the blonde one eventually knocked at my side door. His accomplices were outside my main entrance. Without alerting him I spoke through the entryphone and tempted him to wait. 'Please hold on for ten minutes. I've just painted my nails and if I open the door right now they will smudge.' I telephoned the police, hoping they would catch the gang red-handed, but they never responded to my call. This infuriated me. How *dare* they ignore something this serious. Fifteen minutes later the three men left, probably moving on to an easier target. These attacks escalated to such an extent that eventually the police had to take notice. The gang were caught and sent to prison.

Violence is a possibility we have to live with daily. Prostitutes working from flats feel safe with male minders at hand, but pimping laws make hiring proper security men impossible. Maids lend an element of security, and they must deter a would-be murderer who doesn't want any witnesses. However, the strongest of maids and a frightened whore are no match for an enraged schizophrenic or psychopathic client. This has been proved many times and not all girls are quick thinking enough to escape. I experienced two incidents where clients were 'not all the ticket'.

The first occasion was in the early seventies. A small Jewish client whom I'd regularly serviced bartered with me on the doorstep. I was wearing a black see-through baby doll nightie, matching frilly panties and black knee-length platform-soled boots. I refused to let him in, and quite unexpectedly he slapped my face and ran off. I was furious and my natural reaction was to chase after him (forgetting I was in baby dolls). I pursued him down Warwick Road, repeatedly shrieking 'Stop thief!', hoping someone would apprehend him. He out-ran my platform boots, but a taxi driver came to my rescue and pinned him against a wall. A crowd of onlookers gathered.

'You've stolen my purse!' I screamed in my attacker's face. But he knew I really meant, 'How dare you hit me, you snivelling little shit!'

The crowd grew thicker and, wanting to get away before someone alerted the cops, he said, 'How much do you want?'

'£10,' I snapped (which I guess would be the equivalent of £100 now). He handed me a tenner from his wallet. 'If I ever see you again, I'll make sure you regret this day,' I warned.

I quickly forgot him until several years later he turned up to see 'Madam Helga'. It's an old trick of the trade (remember Australia?) for whores to occasionally don wigs and fake accents in a ruse to pretend they're a 'new girl'. This way, ex-clients who didn't like them return for the 'other mistress' and you have the chance to be nice and win them back. For three months I went through a phase of being 'Madam Helga', a disciplinarian from Hamburg, wearing a long black wig, dark make-up, jack boots and Nazi armbands.

When he knocked, I recognised him through the spy hole, and immediately hatched a plan with my maid. She let him in, took his fee for domination (it's common for maids to take the punter's fee), and asked him to undress. 'Madam Helga's very kinky. She likes her slaves to wait in the pillory.' She urged him to place his head and hands into the medieval punishment contraption, then she snapped it shut and locked it. Speaking with a sexy German accent, I entered the dungeon.

''Allo, boy! I vant you to pay attention. Vatch me very closely.' Then I took off my wig and changed my voice back to Cockney. 'Huh! Remember me?'

He was frightened. He was trapped! I selected my longest, swishiest cane, and whacked his arse non-stop until he apologised for hitting me, and explained his reasons. 'I'm sorry, I was like a spoiled kid who couldn't get my own way.' I took his photograph and told him I would circulate it amongst the girls, so no-one would see him again. It's not often that whores get their own back on nasty clients, but this was one of them.

One of my safety precautions is to purposely have ill-fitting doors which don't shut. In this way, any would-be assailant can't trap you inside a locked room. This came in handy on the second occasion a dangerous punter came my way. He had called for a simple hand

Left: Aged 19, lining up for Madame's daily inspection in the Paris brothel. I was wearing the diamond and sapphire jewellery Ernst had given me.

Below: Age 17, Hell's Angel 'Lady Scratch'. *Roger Phillips*

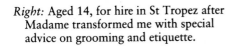

Right: Aged 14, for hire in St Tropez after Madame transformed me with special advice on grooming and etiquette.

Madam of my own opulent brothel, and loving every minute of it. *Syndication International*

In my Crucifix Dungeon. *'All my clients have a cross to bear!'*
Syndication International

Left: Making a Corrective Party election broadcast. *'Eat your heart out big boys, the Correctives will outshine you.'*

Right: Outside our party headquarters, being interviewed by the Russian media.

relief, and I put him in my rubber room (the most convenient room at the time), pushing the door to for privacy. He seemed quite content lying on the rubber-sheeted bed, and there were no bad vibes at all (usually you can sense a dodgy atmosphere and act accordingly). I sat beside him and gave a quality service to which he reacted quite normally. Then after he'd ejaculated he suddenly, without provocation, lunged at me quite menacingly, repeating 'I know you! I know you!' I leapt up and fled into the street through one of my numerous emergency exits (another safety precaution) before he had a chance to grab me.

I ran down Penywern Road (the adjoining street) and knocked on the door of another whore, Sue. I telephoned my maid and told her what had happened. Sue had a Rottweiler dog trained to attack on command and maul the genital area. She accompanied me back, with intentions of setting her dog on him. However, in the meantime, my maid had found him dressing as if nothing had occurred. She humoured him – 'That's a nice shirt' – and offered him a cigarette (kept as a prop for such occasions). He went without a problem, obviously a schizophrenic. But if I hadn't escaped, who knows what might have happened!

A similar scenario must have occurred with Elly, a young black American whore working relief (when the regular whore takes time off and sublets her flat) in Soho. At approximately 2.40 am on Friday, 15 May 1992, she received a client who paid for his service, got undressed, then slashed her throat with a Stanley knife. On hearing the screams, her maid ran to her rescue, but was knocked to the floor. The 'Newman Street Ripper', as we now call him, ran naked into the street, clutching his blood-spattered clothes. When the maid came to, she took off her skirt and wrapped it round Elly's neck. If she hadn't been at hand to summon help, Elly would have bled to death.

This is yet another statistic to add to my compilation of prostitutes attacked and murdered in the past fifty years. Many thousands have been throttled, hacked and bludgeoned to death. But the account I still find most horrid is when twenty-seven-year-old Catherine Russell was stabbed to death by a client in the Savoy Hotel, London, at 10 pm on 1 October 1980. Her murderer told police: 'I just wanted to kill a prostitute.'

Brutality towards prostitutes is one of the 'enemies' of the trade, but even that seemed trivial compared to AIDS. Government propaganda in the mid eighties encouraged well-established Mistresses, like myself, to consider early retirement. I felt sorry for the whores lower down the ladder who continually spent their entire earnings on drink, drugs and pimps, leaving no savings to fall back on. They needed to carry on working, regardless of the dangers. Whenever a prostitute died of AIDS (and to date I know of thirty-four instances from among my own group of friends) the news buzzed around the grapevine and we organised small church services amongst ourselves to pay tribute. What I found alarming were the rumours that death certificates stated another cause of demise. Although I understood the next-of-kin's need to avoid the stigma of AIDS, it meant incorrect medical statistics were being gathered by the authorities.

I became obsessed about hygiene during those first frightening years of AIDS awareness. I'd always been fussy anyway, and insisted my clients refrained from touching their penis once I'd put a condom on it (men have a habit of wiping their cocks with their hands). I didn't want any germs transferred from their dirty hands on to my clean condom. I also refused to let them 'put it in' themselves because they were rough – they didn't care if their nails split the rubber – and risk was minimised if I guided their members home myself.

Millions of pounds were spent on ads promoting safe sex with a condom, but I kept thinking, what if one broke! Three had broken in the past, and they were the best-known brand. And what about cunnilingus? A man with gum disease (pyorrhoea or bleeding gums) could easily spread HIV when sucking a woman, especially if there was broken skin on her vagina. My long nails had occasionally scratched when inserting tampons, so I recognised the danger and refused to receive oral sex unless it was through a sheet of clingfilm.

Two Scottish prostitutes told me they worked without condoms even though they had full-blown AIDS. Their attitude was that 'If men want to take the risk, it's their look-out.' They each serviced 100 men a week which added up annually to 10,400 men at risk. It's quite usual for clients to travel all over the country to see whores, and the thought of HIV-infected clients visiting me made me even more paranoid.

At first I insisted my clients wore two condoms (one on top of the other), even for a wank. But the anxiety made me bite my nails which left broken skin round my fingertips. Germs could enter, so I wore latex surgeon's gloves as a 'double' protection. I considered sperm to be my enemy. Even when a regular client whom I fancied made love to me I would cringe half-way through and push him off. To keep clean I had always taken Dettol baths between clients, but as my paranoia grew I began bathing with full-strength industrial disinfectant. (The first time it burnt my skin off – I had to dilute it.) After work I couldn't bring myself to empty the waste-bins which were full of used condoms. So I ended up buying lots of cheap wicker waste-baskets for £1 each so at the end of the day I could simply throw them out complete with contents.

Eventually I rejected straight sex altogether and refused mouth to body contact. The only clients I was prepared to service were those seeking verbal domination, correction or bondage, on the clear understanding that they didn't touch me and they wanked themselves off whilst I stood out of 'splash-shot'. Excited clients always dripped with sweat or sprayed saliva during kinky dialogue, and I considered all bodily fluids to be contaminated. I even rejected clients who were thin or spoke with an American accent because I'd read that AIDS caused weight loss and was rife in the States. This was unfortunate for my libido because, apart from earning money, the best thing about being a whore was having multiple orgasms on demand.

I needed to find a lover without risk of disease, and I felt the safest sex of all was lesbianism – after all you can't get AIDS from a dildo. So I resumed socialising with Chris and Agnes and Biff and Tracy. Agnes and I became rivals. We were the same colouring, height and age, and both extrovert nymphomaniacs. She flaunted her fabulous 36-22-36 figure; I flaunted my substantial estate. Agnes was a first-rate 'drama queen': she would slash her wrists, take overdoses, put her head in the gas oven and jack up on heroin all at the same time. Frequently, she would disappear for weeks on end to screw as many people as possible. Besotted Chris said, 'If you want someone and they're full of shit, then you just have to put up with it.' Agnes had threatened to kill Chris many times, and on one particularly frightening occasion we reported the threat to the Acton police, but were dismissed as sexual perverts with trivial domestic problems.

Meanwhile, the fetish and fantasy business at Earl's Court continued to flourish. There were lots of parties, the most outrageous were held around Christmas or on Bonfire Night. At Christmas we would decorate naked slaves with fairy lights and prickly holly! The parties were always run the same way, entry by invitation only, and men had the option of hiding their identity under ski masks. I could cram over 200 people into the house in Eardley Crescent. Sometimes I'd have lower-key parties without VIPs for members of the media and underworld figures.

Once a client was helping to tidy up after a party and drank all the leftovers. He passed out. A slave who liked to be dragged along the floor (as I said, they all had their individual peculiarities!) helped me drag the unconscious man out into the street. We left him propped up by a lamp-post whereupon my slave said: 'He's getting *my* service, Madam, and he hasn't even paid for it!' (The drunk was still there an hour later, and I called 999. He was taken to St Stephen's Hospital in Fulham, his stomach pumped out, and kept overnight for observation. God knows what he told his wife! I barred him from the House of Fetish and Fantasy from then on.)

Attendance at parties in Acton was limited to twenty carefully selected guests, and involved the swimming pool. This had finally been installed, but only after a couple of disasters. There was a problem with the first builder, and then I went on a cruise, leaving 'Butch John', one of my temporary lesbian lovers, with the first instalment of £2,000. This she spent on riotous living – champagne all round for her cronies at one of the gay clubs, for instance. The pool was finally finished, though, with a bar, jacuzzi and sun-bed, all enclosed in Swiss pine and glass with window boxes. We had orgies in the pool, and a special game for 'rubber kinks'. One of the men would be put into an inflatable rubber cocoon and floated into the middle of the pool. Then the female guests threw dice. The highest number won the pleasure of popping the rubber with a sharpened number 10 knitting needle. It then deflated and the man inside found it extremely difficult to stay afloat, and went down flapping layers of rubber. Part of his pleasure, of course, was to be humiliated, and we'd all jeer at him for sinking. I supervised all of this, floating around naked in a rubber dinghy, drinking champagne and cracking a whip.

I went to work at Eardley Crescent every day. Shelley was still my maid and we continued to play Kaluki while the clients 'suffered', until disaster struck. Shelley had a brain haemorrhage. Having seen someone die of this a few years earlier, I recognised the symptoms at once and rushed her to St Stephen's Hospital. They said she was too *'compos mentis'* to have had a brain haemorrhage, and sent her home with an aspirin. There she was in such diabolical pain, she was rushed to Hammersmith Hospital where they gave her an emergency operation. This experience brought home to me how overworked and underpaid workers in the National Health Service are, and I resolved to do something about it as soon as I could. Shelley underwent a long convalescence. I had to carry on with other maids and we drifted apart.

Unfortunately, I was eventually diverted from my work at the House of Fetish and Fantasy by a new relationship. I took up with Biff who was Dyke of the Day, therefore a natural target for me. (I always had to have the best; even when I was with the Hell's Angels, I had to be the leader's girl.) Biff was a dark-haired ruffian who was reputed to be the best pussy sucker on the gay scene, and all the feminine lesbians wanted her. She was down on her luck, having recently been nicked for clipping, so it was easy to lure her into a relationship; one flash of money and this handsome slim dyke was all mine.

She had a black belt in karate and entertained me by tearing up telephone directories, chopping bricks in half and doing fancy press-ups. She claimed to be the illegitimate daughter of the late William Hill (the bookmaker), and as our relationship blossomed she had me traipsing all over Newmarket, spying on his relatives at their stud farm. She was crude and constantly slagged men off. 'It's their dirty cocks that give women cervical cancer,' she said (which recent medical research has corroborated). She was ultra fastidious and bragged that because she'd never been with a man her body was a 'germ-free zone'. In the past (before AIDS) she insisted that all her previous 'wives' were tested for sexually transmitted diseases like syphilis, gonorrhoea, thrush, chlamydia, herpes and trichomoniasis before she touched them. I did the same, and naturally the results were negative.

But I had jumped out of the frying pan into the fire because life with Biff was far worse than with Val. She took over, rearranging my house and throwing out photographs of special clients displayed around my bedroom. She was jealous and sat outside Eardley Crescent spying, accusing me of having affairs with anyone who stopped longer than half an hour. Once, when I'd had rare sex with a punter (a civil servant, of whom more later), she went berserk. 'You've let a "man" contaminate you!' She smashed up the house and refused to make love with me until I'd taken ten baths in disinfectant. Even then she over-reacted: 'Urgh. You smell of men.' Then she looked into the bath and said 'Urgh, that's work water.'

I felt safe from AIDS during this time with Biff, and at work I still applied strict hygiene rules. One day, however, I was caning a man's bottom when his skin split. His blood spurted up and hit me in the eye. I freaked out! I left him tied over the whipping bench and ran outside dressed in a PVC catsuit and thigh-length waders. I hailed a cab to St Stephen's Hospital to take an AIDS test. The doctor assured me I couldn't get AIDS in this way, but I wasn't taking any chances. When I got home, two hours later, the client I'd abandoned was enjoying his extra time in bondage, and was happily waiting for more caning. Not in the mood, I released him and refunded his money. I threw my bloodstained whips and canes into the dustbin and waited three miserable weeks for the test results – it was like waiting on Death Row. The result was negative, but nevertheless it was one scare too many. I decided to give up work altogether.

From then on I invested my cash on the money market to ensure an income (I was always business minded), and I spent the next two years pandering to Biff's every whim, buying her expensive presents and feeding her at fancy restaurants along King's Road. To ensure I didn't return to work, Biff dismantled my dungeons with a chainsaw and threw the bits of equipment out into a builders' skip. She reduced my House of Fetish and Fantasy to a pile of rubble, but left the bedrooms intact. These I rented out as furnished bed-sits, keeping the basement for a town flat. Some of the wood from the torture racks became the base of the kitchen cabinets. All this work necessitated removing the stairs: over the years, those stairs have been changed about six times.

We carried on living in Acton on my savings, but I was uneasy with that house. I'd already lost my jewels in a robbery prior to the lesbian relationships. Someone had taken my key. I'd left my diamonds spread around in pyrex dishes, mostly loose stones which were being assembled for a jeweller to make into spectacular drop earrings. When I came back from a day out in Scotland, they had gone.

My one consolation was that the robber hadn't found my cash. I made a practice of accumulating £1,000 at a time which I called 'a bundle'. This went into an envelope and was hidden in the bottom of my pianola. There were twenty of them tucked down there the day of the robbery. However, I had at least £30,000 worth of diamonds and I had my suspicions. I called in the police who shrugged it off as an occupational hazard. Suspicions were not enough. This made me furious. Prostitute or not, it was my right to expect police assistance, but nothing more was done. Eventually this would become part of my election manifesto, and 'public accountability of the police' is now proving to be a necessity.

Because of this and the emotional dramas and rows caused by my lesbian partners, I was sure there was an evil presence in my house. I decided to have it exorcised by one of my regular punters, 'The Gas-Mask Vicar'. He protested that he was hardly qualified, but I insisted he at least have a try. It didn't seem to work.

The rows between Biff and me went on, so I decided to sell. The house went for £93,000, less than market price, but I was more worried about what the new owners might do to my American bull-frogs who lived in the fountain-topped fish-pond. During one of the lulls in our fighting Biff and I went on a rescue mission. We scooped the frogs out into a bucket and took them in the Jag to Longford where they were let out into a leafy tributary of the Thames. They must be a big colony by now.

My relationship with Biff was built around sex and money, there was no mental stimulus, and I began missing my clients' intellectual conversations on finance, medicine, law, politics, current affairs and languages. (One client had taught me how to say 'Want to fuck?' in fifteen different languages!) I had always received fan mail (including 64 proposals of marriage) and the volume increased as desperate clients urged my return to business. Biff began intercepting the post. She accused me of encouraging 'perverts and prospective rapists' and to punish me she slept with other women, making me jealous, which led to even more fights (including one with Ava Motley, an actress who had made good in 'The Widows' TV series).

Gradually our sex life deteriorated, and when the house in Acton was sold, Biff got herself a council flat in Muswell Hill where she occasionally kept other women on 'my' money. I became obsessed and spent £90,000 buying a nearby property just so I could spy on her. (I later used it as a safe house for prostitutes trying to escape men who brutalised them, having founded an underworld organisation called HELP, Harlots Escaping Licentious Pimps. Quite a few young whores stayed there, all with the same pathetic background –

abused as kids, runaways selling sex for survival. They hadn't a clue how to get off the game. I became the Erin Pizzey of battered prostitutes and still am. One day, I will register my safe house as a charity.)

I even bugged Biff's phone, and had her followed by private detectives. None of my other friends liked her, but I hated them saying 'I told you so'! I tried Chris's philosophy, 'If you want someone who's full of shit, then you have to put up with it.' So in an attempt to hold on to her, I moved into her flat. I gave her money to decorate it, but she frittered it away. I bought her a black Mercedes 450 SL convertible, but she flaunted long-legged bimbos in it so I took it back. Her ex-girlfriends hung around like vultures waiting to take my place. On reflection, Biff was like a drug habit – expensive, destructive, and difficult to give up.

I even tried being dramatic to see if she'd miss me. I took off to Nevada, then phoned with an ultimatum: 'Either you behave or I'm not coming home.' 'Stay there then,' she said, and hung up. To take my mind off the emotional turmoil I went to a chicken ranch (a brothel in the desert) where, after introducing myself, I was welcomed like a long-lost friend. The set-up was unique, fifteen trailers parked in a circle with a barbed-wire fence around the outside, and I worked there for a week (it was reputedly underworld controlled). I moved on to Las Vegas and picked up playboys at the blackjack tables. They thought nothing of paying 2,000 dollars a time for an 'English lady'. I made a small fortune which I spend on a diamond bracelet when I stopped off in Hong Kong en route to London.

As a last-ditch attempt to make Biff realise she could lose me I bought a can of orange Fanta and 100 paracetamol and took an overdose. She called an ambulance which rushed me to Brook Hospital for my stomach to be pumped. The nurses slagged me off for wasting National Health time and I felt totally humiliated and ashamed. To this day I cringe at the sight of green rubber aprons, white plastic jugs, funnels and rubber hoses. It was a nightmare! I was violently sick for a week, as I had given myself jaundice. Apparently paracetamol destroys the liver, and overdosing on it is the most painful way to go. I was kept in for five days' observation and Biff never visited me once.

That was when I threw in the towel and decided to return to work. In all I had wasted about seven years on the gay scene; frittered away tens of thousands of pounds; and I had abandoned my special clients, some of whom I genuinely loved. (Biff and I, despite our differences, agreed to stay friends and it was rather amusing in February of 1992 when she came to testify as a witness in a court case. She is still with the blonde bimbo who ultimately replaced me, and we all went out for a meal afterwards. It was like a scene in a modern play, the 'ex wife' and the present 'wife', still all good friends.)

Conveniently, as Biff and I broke up, the rental agreements of the furnished rooms in Eardley Crescent were up. I realised Earl's Court was where I belonged. The house underwent another reconstruction to put me back in business full time. Doors were changed and yet another set of stairs installed. The dungeons were rebuilt and a new 'medical' room fitted out, based on my stay in hospital.

Back in my old life with customers who were delighted to see me, and needed me, I was happier. It took a while to get over the breakup with Biff, though. My new maid, another lesbian called Sybil, tried to help by befriending me. We would go out together for meals, and her friends dropped by to cheer me up. One of them was a butch lesbian who lived as a man and worked for an undertaker. Sometimes he/she would pop in for tea on the way to a funeral, leaving the hearse outside, complete with coffin, which rather bewildered passers-by!

Sybil flirted with me constantly, but I didn't respond. I saw our relationship strictly as business, with the welcome addition of friendship. We were both strong characters and inevitably our relationship deteriorated as we rowed over money and property. On one occasion I got so angry with her that I went to her flat armed with a 'handbag size' aerosal of CS gas, planning to knock her out. She called the police and I hid the spray in a neighbour's flowerpot. I heard afterwards that the neighbour had found it, and had tried out the fragrance!

Soon after this I took off for a five-week world trip to get tanned. I wanted to look good in my leopard-skin loincloth (my favourite work outfit). Charlie, my minder, insisted on driving me to the airport and whilst we were preparing to depart, two punters knocked. 'Sorry, I only take one at a time.' They hovered for a while, desperate to come in, but when they saw Charlie they suddenly changed their minds and ran away. I thought nothing of it.

This turned out to be a lucky escape because they weren't clients at all. Their names were Robert Causadon-Vincent and Barry

Parsons, both assassins hired by Agnes. She and Chris had finally split up, on very bad terms, and wanting revenge – although it was nothing to do with me – Agnes had instructed two thugs she knew to steal my valuables and murder me.

Their next step was Chris who, unfortunately, was working alone, a very dangerous thing to do. She opened the door and consequently suffered the most horrific ordeal imaginable. She was a strong woman and put up a desperate fight, so the police said. Robert and Barry robbed, raped and buggered her, crushed her throat with an iron bar, trussed her body up like a chicken, and drowned her in a blood-soaked bath. This was my first close friend to get murdered.

The tabloids sensationalised it with headlines like 'Miss Whiplash Garotted at Torture Den' and 'Love Feud Bath Murder'. Everyone thought it was me! At the time, I was sunning myself on Brampton Island off the Great Barrier Reef, and when my relief Mistress, Black Donna, telephoned to break the awful news, I thought instantly of Chris and me speaking to Seth on the *ouija* board. He had warned me of murder, but the warning should have been for Chris.

Agnes and her two henchmen were tried at the Old Bailey in 1986. The public gallery was jam-packed with prostitutes, but I didn't go – I was too upset. It was a week-long revelation of sordid sex, sick, twisted emotions and violence. Robert and Barry revealed that Agnes had also sent them to my Acton house, but I had already moved. The men got life, Agnes got seven years for manslaughter, but she was later acquitted on appeal. Word went out that someone put a contract on Agnes and that she was to suffer exactly the same fate as Chris, but she never came back into circulation. Whilst in Holloway prison she had an affair with a screw, and on her release they both fled to Spain.

I blamed the police for the death. If they hadn't ignored us when we reported Agnes' previous threats, Chris would still be alive today. This to me was yet another example of the police treating prostitutes as second-class citizens. I felt very strongly that this shouldn't be so, and, as I recovered my spirits, I determined to do something about it. My sense of the injustice of it all was growing, and the possibility of political action began to beckon even more urgently. First, though, I had to face another problem.

8

The Taxman Cometh

I first heard from the Inland Revenue way back in 1977, their interest in me stemming from a tip off from a transvestite tax inspector. His main fantasy was to dress up in ladies' clothes and get hand relief, but he also required extras like a bit of bondage and verbal correction. Over the years, this punter had been over-indulged and spoiled, being charged only about £5 while the other punters were already paying £15. Even at that price, he'd bait me down to £4. After a while, I got annoyed and said if he didn't start paying full price per session, he could no longer come to me.

He was furious: 'You money-grabbing bitch, you haven't paid any tax, have you? You'll regret this day!'

There's nothing worse than a vindictive pervert. He turned out to be more damaging than any bent copper I'd ever had to deal with.

I received a letter from the Tax Office. 'We don't appear to have you on our files. Would you kindly fill in the enclosed forms?' Since anybody taking immoral earnings from a prostitute is guilty of pimping, which is illegal, I, like others of my kind, did not expect or recognise that we could be liable for tax. Most prostitutes lead anonymous lives anyway. There is no record of them, nor will they come forward for fear of being victimised.

I ignored the forms I received and wrote a letter to the Tax Office: 'If brothel keeping is to be recognised and taxed, then will my brothel convictions be quashed and my fines refunded?'

They ignored this and sent me more assessment forms.

I sought advice from a tax specialist who had been recommended to me. He had a seedly little office and charged me £2,000 at the rate of £200 an hour, a fortune in the seventies. He claimed he had spent several hours studying my paperwork, but I still felt exploited. It seemed that in my trade I could never escape greedy people who felt they could rip me off.

Dissatisfied with this man, I remembered an article in one of the tabloids about a prostitute called Helen Buckingham who was threatened with bankruptcy. She too had been shocked by her tax demand. The general understanding among prostitutes was that their fines were their way of paying tax. The paper had named her accountant as Dennis Gilson. He was a Trustee in Bankruptcy for Richard John Bingham, the Seventh Earl of Lucan. For once, a different kind of 'Dennis' was to enter my life, one in whom I saw no danger.

I made contact, and we had a preliminary chat, but I was still a little wary because of the earlier encounter with the tax specialist. I also thought I might still be able to handle this tax situation on my own.

A letter arrived from the Inland Revenue demanding an affidavit and details of my business affairs and assets since 1975. I suspected they were trying to catch me out so that they could accuse me of fraudulently avoiding taxes. Shortly after this, a telephone call came from the Inland Revenue; a randy civil servant was offering to help me with this current problem in return for sex.

First impressions when 'Spy' arrived at the house in Acton were not favourable. He was fat and stunk of BO. Very familiarly, he suggested I sit next to him on the sofa to help me recall to date all that had taken place between me and the Inland Revenue.

He had brought a copy of my 'case file' to refresh my memory, and advised me not to admit to illegal brothel keeping.

'The Inland Revenue work hand in glove with the police,' he warned. 'They will report you and have you nicked.'

He advised that I put 'prostitution' as my sole profession because it was legal. (I later regretted doing this – it rendered my future argument about taxation on illegal brothels totally irrelevant.) He wrote out my affidavit, telling me to copy it in my own handwriting and destroy his original. (However, I kept his original and still have it.)

He was repulsive, but I didn't renege on the deal. I made him shower, then gave him sex. (It was after this encounter that I had one of my worst rows with Biff.)

I then consulted with Dennis the accountant again. He told me that my tax assessment amounted to £110,000, which to me was unbelievable. He negotiated it down to £46,000 which he felt was a good result, and said that I should pay up. I didn't agree; no consideration had been given to the costs of the girls working in my brothel, or the expense of employing maids and minders. An appointment was made for my premises to be inspected so that they could see how I worked.

Two men from the Inland Revenue Special Office came round to Eardley Crescent. To make the visit as uncomfortable as possible for them I had four other prostitutes present. I walked around topless, one girl was totally naked, the others were in bizarre black leather outfits. We took them on a tour of the rooms exchanging crude comments while holding up embarrassing items like sanitary towels and haemorrhoid cream to question whether they were tax-deductible. We even asked if a tonsillectomy would be tax-deductible because it aided oral sex.

They asked for explicit details – how I worked, what services I provided, how long each client stayed etc. Then they wanted to see my appointments diary, my clientele list, my cash books and business invoices to corroborate any expenses I might wish to offset against my income.

'I don't keep a diary or clientele list,' I protested. I *did* really, but I was damned if I was going to let them know the identity of my clients. I explained that prostitutes aren't given invoices for equipment because people who make racks, pillories, stocks, gallows, whips and other torture gadgets are secretive. They come on site, sell the gear, then disappear without leaving their names, numbers or receipts. It's a case of 'don't call us – we'll call you'. Minders don't give receipts either; they're part of the underworld, and similarly I couldn't reveal their identities.

The tax inspectors made it clear – 'No receipts, no tax deductions!' – which meant my enormous running costs wouldn't be recognised and I'd be taxed on gross income, not net profit.

They even said that cash gifts from boyfriends were taxable which I found a little extreme. After all, millions of women's lovers give them cash to buy presents for themselves, and they're not taxed on it. I felt victimised, as if the State were making an example of me.

The two men were there all afternoon.

Fortunately, by now I had learned to manipulate the Press and had tipped them off in advance about the Inland Revenue visitation. A selection of them turned up early, parking opposite, with zoom lenses poised from car windows. Some even hid behind my garden wall for a better shot. I laughed as one embarrassed tax inspector held his newspaper in front of his face to avoid being photographed; the other hid behind his briefcase.

Carol Barnes, then an up-and-coming TV news reporter, turned up with a camera crew. She sat on my bed and interviewed me in my 'dressing-up' room. I recounted the Inland Revenue Special Office's 'time and motion' study of my profession. I thought the subject merited extensive exposure. It was hypocritical that prostitutes were criminalised by a government which craftily levied taxation on them at the same time.

Inspired by my predicament, the *Daily Star*'s cartoonist captured the hypocrisy perfectly. His depiction was of binocular-bearing tax inspectors lusting at my brothel door. The caption read: 'We'd like to take a closer look at your figures.'

The 'Special Office' is the Inland Revenue's Gestapo. They left no stone unturned in their efforts to bleed me dry. Like a banker, doctor or lawyer observes a code of confidentiality, so do I, as all prostitutes should! And luckily for clients who'd paid by cheque, I had the foresight to protect their identities from snoopers investigating my banking records. A cautious move, which I'd learned from Jake's father, was to request that my deposit slips were returned to me after they'd been processed. This prevented the discovery of names and sort codes which were itemised on my deposit vouchers. Also I had my own personal cheques returned to me from the clearing house, because sometimes, if I had accidentally double-booked my girls, I sent refund cheques to clients who had pre-paid their fees. Removing such evidence from the bank ensured my customers' identities were protected. Such 'sensitive' banking records, diaries and cashbooks were kept in my safety deposit box and were unavailable for inspection.

Because the tax inspectors were unable to scrutinise my bank vouchers, they nit-picked at everything on my statements, demanding confirmation of payees and items purchased. There was no concealing the fact that a fortune had flowed through my account, and despite my explaining that a significant portion of the money

" Er ... VAT ... we'd like to take a closer look at your figures."

was held by me as trustee for several girls, they wouldn't believe me without my revealing the girls' identities – and that too was against my code of practice.

Many prostitutes fritter their money away, leaving nothing for their retirement. As a precaution against this, it was the norm, at the request of the girls, for the Madam to look after their earnings. If ever they wanted to buy something specific, I gave them a cheque made payable for the relevant amount. Otherwise I simply totted up their balance and wrote 'Not to exceed £— (their balance)' on the bottom of the cheque. I always encouraged my girls to save and prosper, as I did.

Thus began a cat and mouse game with the tax authorities which was to cover many years. It's still going on!

Meanwhile, at my accountant's suggestion, I formed a company to regulate my business affairs. Determined to be totally honest, I called it 'Prostitution Limited'. This was rejected by Companies House as 'undesirable'. I tried 'French Lessons Ltd' and 'Hookers Ltd'. Both were rejected. The Registrar finally accepted 'Lindi St Clair, Personal Services Ltd'. (This was long before the film about

Cynthia Payne entitled *Personal Services*.) Specifically written into the Company Memorandum of Association was the trade of 'prostitution' but, six months later, the Attorney General struck off the company in a court hearing. He said it was against public policy to have a company for immoral purposes.

I had no chance to challenge this because the telegram notifying me of the date of the hearing had been sent to 55 Eardley Crescent instead of 58. For the moment, I was rather taken by the name of the case: 'The Queen versus Lindi St Clair'. So I was forcibly deregistered, and the company was deemed not to exist. Needless to say, I'm not finished with my argument. If prostitution is a trade in the eyes of the Inland Revenue, I should be entitled to have a limited company.

There was vast media coverage following this deregistration. I was christened 'Miss Whiplash' – the automatic name given to any whore who caters for sexual flagellation. Sensationalist, I know, but I didn't mind – I found it quite befitting. And after that the name just seemed to stick!

About this time, Thames Television started preparing a documentary on five prostitutes. They wrote to all the whores in kinky sex contact magazines. (I advertised in many, and made the front cover of one once, *Superbitch*.) I was Thames's top-level choice: the others were a low-class whore of thirty-five who did travelling salesmen; a young one who had a violent pimp; an older, ex-society whore who'd gone broke; and a middle-class, middle-aged whore who lived on the coast. I was twenty-eight then, and the only one who said she enjoyed her work.

They filmed me in the opulent surroundings of the house in Acton, then in my Jag talking on the car phone, something which was still unusual and very expensive. The viewers heard me ordering diamonds, and then the camera followed me to the Mayfair jeweller to buy them with my credit card. The programme stirred up a lot of media comment, one reporter saying I lived like Hugh Hefner of *Playboy*. It also stirred up a lot of jealousy with rival prostitutes. They sabotaged my property and possessions. They vandalised my car and put superglue in the locks of the house – imagine, a busy day, a queue of randy men, and the brothel door glued shut!

Later, what with all this arguing about the company and my tax problems, the attention of the media was focussed on me yet again. I received an invitation to be on the Janet Street-Porter show,

'Around Midnight'. They offered me £50. I said I wanted a grand. They refused. I settled for £500. I'll admit now that I'd have done it for £50 for the excitement and glamour.

Waiting in the Green Room to go on, I met the author Martin Amis and Lord Kinsdale, who was there to talk about working as a bingo caller and a plumber. I presented him with a way he could improve his situation: 'Fancy getting married?' It seemed a fair swop to me. He'd have my money, and I'd have his title. I was ignored! (I offered to have a baby for the heirless Duke of Atholl recently; that too was ignored!)

I drank the warm white wine on offer and thought of a more immediate way of getting attention, and when called on stage, I took an empty wine bottle to whack the bums of the camera crew. Then I joined the assembled panel, which included Auberon Waugh, and we discussed kinky houses in relation to a current news story about a holiday villa in Spain. It had been reported that couples paid to be kept there in dog kennels. I spoke about similar clients who visited my House of Fetish and Fantasy, as well as some of the other sexual quirks I fulfilled for them.

This appearance became the start of invitations from various forms of the media worldwide. They sought my opinions and advice on subjects related to my work: a prostitute being murdered; a public figure caught kerb crawling; a household name, male or female, rumoured to be gay (I don't, however, indulge in such gossip); any court cases involving sado-masochism or pornography; legal reform or general research into prostitution. I was once in a heated debate with an academic who had researched some prostitutes. He was unable to recognise that I knew the subject from ground level and could therefore speak with far more authority!

I'm still being asked my views on various subjects. Quite recently the *Independent* quoted my response to the proposition that men were more ignorant about the workings of their own bodies than they were about women's. Few men know about prostate disease, for instance, although one in three can expect to suffer from some form of it. Many men I've seen have had a swelling of the testicles, and they just think their balls have grown. I've diagnosed a hernia and sent them off to the doctor, and they've come back and thanked me.

My tax situation dragged on, and highlighted double standards. The system was so unfair. I was barred from registering a company, penalised for trading, and yet the Inland Revenue were demanding I pay tax. As a protest, I refused unless I was mercantile (allowed to advertise and rent premises, like any other tax-paying trader). This is a phrase I'd learned from one of my legal advisers and which is used by people in the know. Lay people find it confusing though, and one transsexual I met thought it meant 'sailors and people in the Merchant Navy'! Unfortunately for me, it didn't. The Inland Revenue began to intimidate me.

To quote Otis James (1725–83), I declared: 'Taxation without representation is tyranny'. The Inland Revenue were unimpressed. They sued me. My advisers were shocked, as were all my clients and colleagues. We thought they had been bluffing. I accused them of pimping.

I dressed conventionally for court in suit and hat. To support me, a pressure group of women picketed outside with placards, and their chanting 'The State is a pimp' got up the nose of the judge. This didn't help – I lost. I scribbled comments on the case across paper aeroplanes, sailing them over the Press. I also wrote a poem about the result of the case, which was printed in the *Sun*:

> 'The judge sat in his crooked wig,
> He seemed against me – what a pig.
> He had arrived two minutes late
> To sum up pimping by the State.
> He ruled I should pay Income Tax;
> I'll get him one day on my racks.'

I appealed against this judgement. I felt this time that if I were to be taxed as a tart, I would appear as one. I arrived at the Law Courts in the Strand in fish-net tights, a low-cut black shiny PVC dress, and steel-studded belt from which handcuffs dangled. It sent the security system berserk. The outfit horrified my barrister who made me cover up with my black mac. Every so often, during the proceedings, my mobile phone rang and I had to duck down behind the benches to take calls from impatient punters waiting to meet me in the Wig and Pen Club opposite the Law Courts. This was not my normal meeting place, but a convenient one in the circumstances.

My barrister claimed, 'To tax what is illegal is fundamentally a violation of the principles of criminal law; in addition, it is "*ultra vires*" to levy tax on a person who cannot be assessed by the statutory power. There is either a statutory power or there is not.' I sat and sketched the interior of the court and the judges (one day, I'm going to have an exhibition of my artistic work).

The QC for the Inland Revenue ruled that prostitution involved the provision of services and was therefore taxable, and this was accepted by the Court. The fact that I was non-mercantile was considered 'irrelevant'. So I lost, and it set a legal precedent, though probably not one welcomed by prostitutes who were too afraid to come out of the closet. An Inland Revenue spokesman was as surprised as I was, and said, 'This is the first time we have got a court decision which says the profits of prostitution are taxable.'

I took my case to the House of Lords – I lost! But I'm not finished yet. My next step will be the European Court of Human Rights. This is a new game I've been drawn into playing, which has already cost me over £15,000 in legal fees.

Despite my tax problems, life had to go on. I splashed out £36,000 on a Rolls Corniche convertible. It was metallic blue with gold fittings. One evening three friends and I, all looking glamorous, were cruising Soho with the top down, looking for a place to eat Chinese. I was flagged down by a policeman who asked to see my documents. There was no reason other than spite, or the fact that he was a 'new boy' looking for a pat on the head from his boss.

My brand-new, personalised licence plate didn't match up with the records when he radioed in. (I'd only just changed them, and the DVLC at Swansea hadn't keyed in the data.) A police van was summoned, and we were all taken off to Vine Street police station. I was accused of grand auto theft, which was ridiculous. My friends were allowed to leave but I was kept in until they could speak to the motor dealer from whom I'd bought the car. I could hear them laughing about the 'high-class tom' they had locked up. Furthermore, they endangered my safety by putting me in a dirty cell with a psychopathic junkie. I asked for the sergeant, as I knew my rights; I was entitled to bail, but never got it. And as if that wasn't bad enough, in towing the Rolls to the police pound, they did £2,000 worth of damage to the bodywork. I had no redress, as it was classified 'within the bounds of duty'.

This incident, on top of all the others, left its mark. I felt very strongly that something needed to be done about such appalling police behaviour. I was determined to find a way. They didn't know it, but what with the taxman and the police – and of course the law itself – I was building up quite a list of injustices and complaints, which in time I'd crusade against.

Another 'venture' at this time was inspired by that aristocratic refusal on the Janet Street-Porter show. For some time I'd been watching the auctions and was also on the Bernard Thorpe (estate-agents) mailing list. They specialised in 'Manorial Lordship' auctions, and I decided if I couldn't marry a lord, I'd be a lady in my own right. I wanted a title beginning with 'L' to match 'Lindi'. Finally I spotted Lot 12, Laxton Manor in the Corby Hundred of Northamptonshire, which dated back to the fifth century and was also recorded in the Domesday Book. The word 'manor' refers to an area, not to any specific building or buildings, and I particularly chose Laxton Manor because it had a history of associations with MPs and beautiful women who followed hazardous pursuits – everything that appealed to me! It had been owned by the 11th Baron Carbery, and it was offered 'together with the village green'.

'Lady Laxton' had a nice ring to it. The bidding started at £2,500 and by the time the price reached £5,000 I was battling it out with only one other person, an American tourist. This made me all the more determined. She gave in at £15,000 and it was mine. I'd paid well over the odds for it, of course, but I didn't care. I was the Lady of the Manor, with a village, population approximately 200, and a village green.

When Christmas came around, I offered £1,000 to help repair the church roof. The bishop sent down word that the money should not be accepted. When the church returned my cheque, the local paper had banner headlines: 'Vice Queen Lindi St Clair Shunned by Church.' This was very unChristian. After all, Jesus forgave Mary Magdalene for prostitution when He met her at the well, and Rahab the harlot was the only person allowed to live when the walls of Jericho crashed down. All I was trying to do was give the church a Christmas present.

I actually think the Church is as hypocritical as the State, and bible bashers continually astonish me with their naïvety, for many churchmen patronise whore-houses. I speak with conviction because amongst my clients there are dozens of vicars and priests, a rabbi, even a bishop. One Irish Catholic priest in particular (whom I call 'The Beast') requires the most deviant sexual game I have ever played, and I must confess it gives me the creeps! For £150, he lies naked on the bed and watches me wrap twelve white sheets around my body, like a Roman toga. Then I slowly strip off, removing one sheet at the beginning, middle and end of each biblical story I recite. Four particular passages excite him. With glazed eyes he masturbates to an incestuous encounter in *Genesis* (20, verses 32–38, where Lot's daughters get their father drunk, have sex with him, fall pregnant and bear his offspring.) Next it's homosexuality in Sodom (*Genesis* 19, verses 1–7); then prostitution (the story of Rahab the harlot in *Joshua* 7, verses 22–25). By this time he is frothing at the mouth and I'm down to my last three sheets. For the finale of this priest's sick fetish, I write the numbers '666' across his chest using scarlet lipstick as I recite *Revelation* 13, verses 16–18 (about the Devil). On reaching the last verse, I stand naked on a chair, glare down at him, my arm outstretched, finger pointing, and I bellow at the top of my voice. *'Here is the wisdom. Let him that hath understanding count the number of the beast: for it is the number of a man; and his number is six hundred, three score and six'*. He ejaculates!

That same Christmas at Laxton, I gave a blank cheque to a local shop to send each villager a bit of seasonal good cheer – a bottle of wine. It wasn't a publicity stunt, I didn't even mention it to the media. I genuinely wanted to give them all something, but some villagers were so outraged they sent the wine back.

Undaunted, with my interest in medieval history I started to arrange a lavish May Day party. I wanted a marquee on the village green with a maypole, village stocks complete with slave for people to throw tomatoes at, and planned on having 200 hookers bussed up from London just to have a good time. The invitation stated: 'Eat, drink and be merry – sumptuous feast, wine, minstrels, jesters, riotous gaiety.'

Suspiciously soon afterwards I received a letter from the local MP, William Powell (Conservative, Corby Constituency), who suggested I'd been upsetting the residents. I was furious. Added to that, I suddenly received a letter from Messrs Farrer and Co., the Queen's solicitors in Lincoln's Inn Fields, who said that the village green had not been for sale along with the lordship of the Manor. I was not to 'claim ownership of their clients' property, or claim to exercise any rights over it'.

I smelled a rat! I've not got to the bottom of it, and to this day I am still trying to unravel the mystery of buying something that supposedly wasn't for sale. Neither my solicitors at the time nor the auctioneers were able to shed any light on it, so I was ripped off yet again – and I don't even know who by.

To get my 'revenge' on William Powell, MP, I had a bit of fun during the 1992 General Election. I invited the Lib Dems to display their poster boards on the green, leaving warnings that if the Tories did the same, I'd send my henchmen up with an axe to chop their boards down.

Meanwhile, I had other problems to deal with like a two-stone weight gain which had given me massive 64″ KK boobs and terrible backache. They may attract clients, but they weigh 14 lbs each! The expensive life I was leading – eating out, receiving gifts of chocolates and crates of champagne and, on a lower level, my insatiable appetite for Hula Hoops which I had delivered by the case – was taking its toll. Despite numerous attempts at dieting, and visits to health farms here and abroad, I'm still a glutton.

9

Entering Politics

During the years that my tax problems hung over me, my political awareness was growing. Not only were the police harassing me, but so were the Inland Revenue, and I knew I had to make my voice heard in some way.

A women's pressure group shared my views, and we attempted a political lobby. Maureen Colquhoun, a Labour MP, put forward 'The Prostitutes' Protection Bill' which would give us more rights. Its first reading passed unopposed in March 1979. Then the General Election brought a change of government. I teamed up with the pressure group, but found them too militant, Marxist and left-wing for my taste. However, it was through them that I was invited to attend a discussion at the Houses of Parliament, chaired by Janet Fookes, MP.

I was very excited by the invitation but my first impression on arrival was how slack the security was: nobody searched me. Perhaps it was because I was so suitably dressed in dark suit and neat low-heeled shoes. I climbed the stone stairs, my eyes and ears like radar antennae, wondering if I would spot any of my clients in the the assemblage below.

'Well, girl', I thought, 'You've come a long way from soliciting lorry drivers!'

The narrow seating area was made up of uncomfortable wooden benches. There was a temptation from my old Hell's Angels days to add my name to those already carved in the back rests, but no, that was in the past. Now I had to behave.

I tried to concentrate on the interpretations of prostitution and punishments, but it was far too dense and boring to hold my attention for long. My thoughts wandered off and I was somewhat startled by a voice: 'Lindi St Clair, what are your views on prostitutes working together?'

Flustered – I hadn't expected this – my mind didn't work fast enough for a clever reply. 'Well, umm, I think it's a good idea. Not only is it not safe for prostitutes to work alone, it's so damn boring. It's nice to have someone to talk to when it's quiet.'

There was a titter round the House at my expense. I was embarrassed for sounding so unprofessional, and cursed myself for not saying more. But this was a new game to me, and I had yet to learn the rules.

My appetite for politics was now aroused, though, and I decided my main concern would be prostitution and the law. No-one could know more about both than I.

Although by now I specialised in kinky punters who didn't require sexual intercourse, I hadn't quite got out of the habit, because I still indulged in straight sex with a chosen few (I was an extrovert nymphomaniac, after all). Some of these men had political connections and as my ambition to effect political change on prostitutes' behalf grew, I knew I needed to be fully cognizant of every aspect of political activity. I knew a bit, but not nearly enough, so from then on, pillow talk was on politics. Clients in bed wanting straight sex were kept on the brink of orgasm until my questions had been answered. If they were of kinky persuasion, I could draw them out during a session of domination; the feeling they had been 'used' made the game even more erotic and kinky for them.

These occasions reaffirmed the hypocrisy and double standards within the British system. Although privately all my influential clients agreed with the decriminalisation of prostitution, none of them had the guts to admit it publicly. What they did suggest was that I should organise a lobby or campaign to get into politics myself. I was constantly being told: 'Anyone can stand for Parliament, even you.'

It was the patronising 'even you' bit that got my goat. I had recognised that I was too young and inexperienced to dare stand for Parliament yet, and resolved that first I would watch, listen and learn. I had already started my campaign to collect as much information as I could. It was quite apparent that none of the main parties so far accepted my theories on legalised prostitution. That got me thinking seriously about other inadequate government policies, particularly those from which I myself had suffered.

As a young schoolgirl, I'd been denied sex education. Thirty years later schools are still without sufficient sex education on the national curriculum. I find it quite shocking that in 1992 people need instruction diagrams for tampons and condoms. While growing up, I'd suffered from inadequate government funding for youth recreational facilities. Things are no better today; riots and vandalism are the voice of the unheard, deriving from total boredom and lack of incentive.

Twenty years ago I was raped. To date, public safety hasn't improved; statistics show that rape occurs every six minutes. Noxious gas anti-rape sprays should be available for women's protection, like 'Mace' (a CS gas spray) which is freely purchased in America and Europe. During my Hell's Angels days, I lived in squalid slums; I'm aghast that over twenty years on, in a supposedly modern civilised society, slums are still abundant and many thousands are homeless.

As a young girl I was bullied and abused by police. In adult life I've experienced fabricated police evidence, corruption and harassment. The police must be made more accountable.

On three occasions I've suffered because of our over-worked and underpaid NHS. Even private health schemes like BUPA and PPP are no help in real emergencies: theres's no time to ring round for private hospital beds when you've suddenly been knocked down by a truck. It was a very busy and harassed NHS doctor who diagnosed Shelley's brain haemorrhage as 'migraine' and sent her home with an aspirin. Once I was left on a trolley, for thirty-six hours, in a hospital corridor whilst I awaited emergency theatre. And on another occasion, when the ambulance staff were on strike, I broke one leg and sprained the other ankle. I was instantly immobilised and needed a stretcher. The hospital told me to take a taxi! Luckily I wasn't somebody without cash or friends to help.

I had lived on both sides of the fence and experienced health and sickness, wealth and poverty, power and powerlessness. Therefore I was well placed to represent the many concerns of the electorate. When the time was right, I would develop my own fringe party and lead it to political victory, fighting for the underdog, and opposing injustices that politicians were too afraid to mention.

I began studying with increasing enthusiasm in and out of bed, and soon discovered that reading political material in libraries bored me stiff. Partly, this was because I wasn't sure what I was looking for. There had to be a better alternative, and I didn't have to look far. I found it in my major talent – pleasing men! – and set about reaching the particular men I needed.

Even though I was well established by then, I still placed massage cards on notice boards – to bring in 'new blood'. Wiser Madams had taught me the importance of 'passing trade', the 'tiddlers' (clients paying minimal rates for a hand job) who are our bread and butter and keep us ticking over. I always hired a local cabby to take me 'carding' because it was too much hassle to drive myself: I hated scrambling for parking spaces outside the shops, and I was too lazy to park up and walk. Stephen, the cabby, kept his motor running whilst I nipped out to pay the ads. I covered one area per week, inserting them for three months, and they were widespread over Greater London. By the time I'd completed my list, three months had expired, and it was time to renew the first batch again. (This was a similar routine to my ex-strip-club circuit.) Most white newsagents were too prudish or scared to accept massage cards, but the Indians gladly took them. Their charges varied, and when the Vice Squad questioned them for living off 'immoral earnings', they would feign ignorance.

Gradually the 'carding' wore me down, so I conjured up an alternative idea, and pioneered a trend for advertising by graffiti. Armed with thick black felt-tip pens, keeping local, I drove to every phone box in Bayswater, Notting Hill and Kensington, and scribbled on the white information panels situated about the phone. For speed, I used short names like Lyn, Liz, Sue, followed by my numbers. I correctly figured that most men when confronted with a provocative message like 'Liz – 373 4848', as they privately used a public phone box, would more than likely dial the number. Curious men called by the dozen, and were lured to my house.

These numbers stayed intact unless vindictive rivals altered their digits. Eventually hundreds of whores followed suit, until there were so many black felt-tip numbers that a client was spoilt for choice. I wanted mine to 'stand out', so I changed tactics and used silver felt tips to write on the black fascias which the panels were fixed to. When others copied, I wrote on the red door frames, the window panes, the grey coin boxes, even on the hand-sets. (In those days, most phone boxes stank of urine, and it's thanks to us girls and our cards that kiosks are frequently cleaned nowadays!)

Keeping one step ahead, I stopped doing numbers and ordered a million white printed stickers which described my figure and services; I stuck these anywhere and everywhere I saw a suitable place to catch the eye. Again others did likewise, but no-one used them more expertly than I in the cause of my political ambitions. By reasoning that the best place to catch an MP's most private attention was when sitting on the toilet, I would have a captive audience.

Stephen lost his taxi-ing job. He had time to kill, so I persuaded him to do 'stickers'. His brother was a political correspondent, prone to gossip, and had often taken Stephen along on official business at Westminster. This, plus Stephen's expert knowledge of London, made him the ideal person to affix stickers on the back of every toilet door in clubs, pubs and restaurants frequented by MPs. I paid him £35 a week to target places within a half-mile radius of Parliament: going north to Trafalgar Square, south to the Tate Gallery, east to Lambeth North tube, and west to Buckingham Gate. He also put stickers on lamp-posts, parking meters, bus stops and road signs.

The message was simple: 'I can do a lot more for you than Maggie can. Call your new sexy Mistress on 373 3344. Try me if you've got the balls.'

I separated my 3344 line from the other work lines. My business interests had now extended beyond the House of Fetish and Fantasy: I had massage ads in the *Yellow Pages*, kinky services on cards in shop windows, and an escort service advertised in magazines (twelve girls on the books). One line was reserved for orders from special clients who wanted souvenir videos of their visit. I also had a private line.

The first call on the 3344 line I received as a result of my sticker campaign was cautious.

'Hello, I saw this number in the men's room. I was curious.'

'Yes, darling,' I said in my best, sexy voice. 'I'm available to escort interesting gentlemen out to dinner and for something more intimate. There's no fee, so this is your lucky day. Would you like to make an appointment?'

'Er . . ., I'll think about it and call you back.'

There was no point rushing anyone. I wanted not only the best, but someone who was serious.

'Fine, I'll look forward to it. Remember, I'll do those naughty things that your other women refused.'

A few days later, he rang again. I recognised the voice. 'Would you like to dine with me tonight?'

This was my first date from the scam. I had no guarantee it would be successful, but was willing to take the chance. A taxi arrived at 8 pm; the driver had been instructed to take me to a very smart hotel. That was fine with me. I was dressed appropriately, mink draped over pink rhinestone-covered cocktail dress (I love glitter). The most important item in my handbag was a notebook. I was prepared for mission number one, which was to learn about politics. For this new game I was about to play, I had chosen the name 'Polly Titian.'

The driver, who told me his first name was 'Dave,' said that he always drove for 'John'. I was asked to wait outside the hotel while he parked, and for a few brief moments, it was like old times, only now I was genuinely waiting – my first real social engagement at one of the top hotels in London! As we went through the revolving doors, Dave gave a discreet nod to a man in his mid-fifties wearing a big smile. He was tall, with brown hair greying at the temples, a nice suit, shiny shoes and clean nails. I was glad to see him so well groomed.

He shook my hand formally. 'I'm glad you've come, would you like a drink?'

'Yes please, Bollinger with lemonade.' I figured as he was going to get a freebie, he might as well learn I had expensive tastes when it came to refreshment.

When we were seated at a table, I studied John's face. It wasn't bad at all. He was obviously doing the same.

'My, you're pretty,' he said.' What's your name?'

'Polly,' I replied,' and I put on a good kettle too.' My sense of humour pleased him and I could see he fancied me rotten. Why not? I had lost a stone straight off my breasts, and my dimensions were now 44D-26-40.

I was still a little concerned that I might be wasting my time with a 'nobody', though he seemed so sure of himself I reasoned he was bound to have some useful advice. I began deliberately and provocatively to find out.

'I bet you'd like to share some fascinating tit-bits with me?'

'Your tit-bits look more interesting than mine.'

This playful routine went on through dinner, dancing and up to a bedroom in the hotel. Four bottles of Bollinger later, I'd learned a little about *Hansard* and a few political snippets. My mind was like a sponge absorbing as much as I could. With a lot of excuses like, 'Darling, pour me another drink – won't be a minute,' I was able to scribble all the information into my notebook in the privacy of the bathroom.

It was all too easy. Men are so egocentric; if there's a young girl sitting on their lap kissing and cuddling, they like to show off.

I spent over six hours with John, much of which aided my research. I decided to nickname him 'Dimple' because he had a dimple on his penis. He had no idea who I really was or that I had an ulterior motive in dating him. I think he asssumed I was a high-class escort girl who left payment to the discretion of the client. He was also flattered to find a pretty young woman interested in his point of view, and my lack of inquisitiveness about his identity made him feel secure.

At 3 am, I prepared to depart and he asked me if I was free that weekend to join him on his boat. I suggested he call me nearer the time. Who knew what other responses I might have had to my stickers by then? The answering machine had been pre-set with an inviting message: 'Hello, I'm the girl of your dreams and if you're man enough, I'll accompany you for dinner and a lot more.'

The call counter showed twelve messages when I got home, but I was too tired to play them back. When the maid woke me some hours later I sent her to the library to pick up the political books that 'Dimple' had recommended and ran off the messages. There were a couple of hopefuls, some heavy breathing and four hang-ups. Interestingly, like lorry drivers, these men all called themselves 'John', but I may have misjudged them. One of the many bits of trivia offered in the run-up to the General Election revealed that anyone called 'John' had a good chance of becoming an MP. That name is in the majority on both sides of the House.

The afternoon after my dalliance with 'Dimple', Interflora delivered a beautiful bouquet of pink roses and a bottle of Bollinger. The unsigned note read: 'Thanks for last night.'

Stephen, my sticker man, arrived for his wages. I was so pleased with the results that I paid him double. He was a political activist at heart, and expanded his 'stickering' to help me capture as many MPs as possible. Over the ensuing months he lurked around the

House of Commons itself, using his brother's position as cover. He discreetly placed stickers behind toilet doors, on wood panelling along the corridors, on radiators, on the legs of the caterers' trolleys, on cupboards, on the trunks of the lime trees in New Palace Yard (the forecourt outside the Members' entrance) and on the black canopy where MPs waited for taxis.

He even managed to stick a few on the Colonnade's Gothic stone arches – a passage leading from Parliament to a security gate at the Bridge Street South side-exit of Westminster Tube. This route, used solely by MPs and others with official passes, was manned by two police officers to prevent unauthorised public wandering from Westminster Tube into private Parliamentary grounds. Stephen waited for a crowd of tourists to mask his actions, then put stickers on the white tile walls next to the gate.

Westminster was only six stops from Earl's Court, a ten-minute tube journey for any randy MP. The more Stephen stickered the vicinity of their work-place, the more chance I had of enticing them along. Obviously my cheeky advertising irritated the Serjeant at Arms and others maintaining public order around the House of Commons, so to avoid getting caught he alternated his 'rounds' and lurked around MPs' offices in Richmond Terrace. Posing as a lost tourist he casually stickered bollards outside numbers 1 to 7. He followed on foot when MPs' cars pulled out from their parking spaces, and turned into Whitehall. The traffic was always choc-a-bloc, which enabled him to sticker their vehicles as he jaywalked across the road.

Sometimes I went with him to sticker eye-catching places around the Ministry of Defence and the Treasury, and I'd amuse myself playing 'spot the MP'. My favourite place for this was Derby Gate and Old Scotland Yard. Once a Labour MP whom I'd occasionally seen on the News brushed past me in Parliament Street; I was taken aback at his lack of height and his bald patch. Such imperfections are always masked on television.

Our luck almost ran out once when a vigilant cop from Cannon Row police station spotted us; we escaped arrest by hiding amidst thick bushes between the terrace of the Whitehall Court and Victoria Embankment Gardens. However I eventually got caught and was fined £25 for bill sticking.

It was apparent that many MPs had business interests in the City, so together Stephen and I did a sticker blitz in the Strand, Chancery

Lane, High Holborn and Grays Inn Road. As we left, men in their thousands – just like ants – flocked over Waterloo Bridge en route to commute home. This prompted me to regularly sticker the train stations at Waterloo, London Bridge and Cannon Street – a sure way to increase my chances of procuring affluent, professional clients.

We managed to get even closer to the heart of Government. When Stephen accompanied his brother into various MPs' offices, he popped my calling cards into any jacket pocket he spied hanging behind doors, on coatstands or draped on chairs. He even sneaked into the House of Lords, placing stickers discreetly in just the right places to catch the political eye. I think by the time he had finished, he had plastered stickers behind every gentlemen's toilet door in SW1. My cheeky campaign came to an abrupt end when I was caught a second time and fined £45 for criminal damage.

Some of the responses to all this activity required men to make several calls before I could convince them there was no charge. They probably ended up thinking that this was a novel way to meet a good-time girl. My procedure echoed advice from Madame in Paris: 'You never ask a gentleman for money, because a proper gentleman will always be grateful and then later, he will feel guilty and always want to give you a present.'

And they did in abundance: the most memorable of which were a cultured pearl choker with ruby pendant, a set of *Encyclopedia Britannica*; a year's subscription to the Wellington Club; and a holiday in Petra which was fabulous. A Master of the Hunt opened an account for me at Swaine & Adeney in Piccadilly so I could buy yellow jodhpurs and other riding gear. He felt I needed to be appropriately dressed to ride on his back, whip him with a crop and dig in with my knees. (I had spurs if needed, but this particular client only liked to be gripped tightly.)

From the responses to the stickers, I averaged about three dates a week. Where we met or ended up depended on what they wanted. It was usually a choice between my luxuriously furnished flat, their hotel or the dungeons. After a few months, I had thirty regular 'boyfriends'. Fifteen of those, including 'Dimple', turned out to be MPs. I added more nicknames to the list, some of which were self-explanatory. They really deserve a separate book!

There was 'Hosepipe', whom I must leave to the imagination, and 'Scarlet', a Labour MP who proved even socialists have their moments. Then there was the grey-haired backbencher whom I call 'Monster' because of his 10-inch penis – it's definitely the largest of the 204 parliamentary penises I've had the pleasure of knowing over the last twenty years. 'Monster' likes to be caned whilst he masturbates into his white linen handkerchief; he says if I don't handle his penis then he feels he hasn't been unfaithful to his wife.

There was also 'Flasher', a Labour backbencher who visited me every six weeks to appease his fetish for indecent exposure. To avoid being recognised, he wore full motorcycle gear – a long oilskin coat, gauntlets, boots and crash helmet – but he was totally naked underneath! Together, we would travel to a remote stop at the end of the Central Line, usually West Ruislip. The idea was to return in separate carriages, and he would repeatedly enter mine and flash at me.

If anyone boarded, we both sat quiet until they alighted. The game continued with 'Flasher' wanking off in the seat opposite me. I would move away, pretending to be disgusted, and he would follow. Sometimes, the train got crowded and we had to travel all the way to Epping at the other end of the line before the game could be completed. 'Flasher' despised police corruption and urged me to identify the tame cop who was under 'Queen's' spell, and who was creaming coke off from drug raids. He promised that under his Parliamentary privilege he could protect his source of information. My strict code of silence prevented me telling him.

'You wouldn't want me to tell on you, would you?'

'Point taken!' he agreed.

There was also 'E', who 'enjoyed' the Wild Wankathon service, and who I watched climb the political ladder, first as a researcher and then into Parliament. His problem was a frigid wife. She had only married him for his fortune and refused any further sexual activity from the moment the marriage was consummated. He was reduced to solo wanking over dirty books, afraid that he was too 'high profile' to approach street prostitutes. When he found my sticker outside Westminster Abbey, he was delighted though still cautious. First he sent a letter on crested notepaper enclosing a £50 note.

'Dear Lindi, I will be in Brompton Cemetery on . . . . Please come to discuss a matter of importance.'

Charlie, my minder, came with me to make sure this wasn't a communication from a dangerous crank. Once I established what

Whips and tits *Richard Loren*

Richard Loren

Right: Drinking and mingling on the House of Commons terrace. *'Eanie, meanie, minie, mo, catch an MP by his toe.'*

Below: 'L' is for Liaison, Lust, Legalise, Libertine, Libel and Loadsamoney.
Syndication International

Updating my Top Drawer mailing list. *'A whore's best friend is her Who's Who – and I'd love to meet Black Rod!'*
Syndication International

was needed, I would travel to Amsterdam to buy magazines of the most explicit nature. I then had to telephone him at a specified time. I imagined him to be in the Members' toilet in the House of Commons with a portable phone, his magazines and clothes pegs. After making sure he was alone, I would launch into a talkathon relating to the sado-masochistic photographs he had gone through and now wanted to copy.

'Look at the picture, start touching yourself. Get nice and stiff for me. Clip your clothes pegs on your nipples. Oooh, isn't that nice? You like the pain, don't you?' . . .

In me he found a discreet way to satisfy his needs, but he annoyed me immensely by returning my magazines with the paper stuck together!

'Horny' was a superfit politician with a soft centre who worked out every day to maintain his lean physique. We first met on Cholmondeley Terrace at the House of Lords during a charity tea party I'd been invited to.

I noticed 'Horny's' adequate inside leg and went out of my way to be introduced. Within seconds I knew he was secretly sexually submissive. There are certain giveaway mannerisms. Just like a doctor can recognise a sick person or a policeman a liar, a Mistress can tell a sexual deviant! I confirmed my theory when he offered to fetch me a drink: 'Does a Mistress have to die of thirst before a compliant male serves her?'

He obeyed without hesitation, a huge swelling filled his fawn trousers. He was later to admit to a secret fascination for dominant, busty women with long red finger nails, and asked to spend the night as my sex slave.

As usual, when I was seeking political advice, the service was gratis. He arrived at 10 pm precisely bearing gifts of *Schofield's Election Law* and the latest edition of the *Parliamentary Companion*, and became my Parliamentary slave. He loved the 'de-spunker' and wanted humiliation. Naked, he acted as a human bench. I sat on his back chirping, 'I've always wanted a political seat' as I flicked through the pages of the books he had brought, occasionally buzzing the 'de-spunker' to give him an extra thrill. Then, I painted my finger nails scarlet and ordered him to blow them dry, one by one. This man had stamina to be admired, not only sexually but politically.

'Lumpy' had risen to back-bench prominence. Little did his

colleagues know that in the course of his fiery speeches, he became so excited that he required my services immediately afterwards.

His fetish was caused by a strict nanny who had spanked him whenever he shouted, and he needed to relive the scenario. What turned him on was the rustling of her underskirts while he was disciplined over her lap. To oblige, I wore a white, high-necked blouse and a long black skirt under which were fifteen starched white net petticoats. He was verbally chastised while his bare bottom was spanked with the back of a wooden hairbrush. He called this 'cherrybumming' because it made his bum cherry red. It also made it very lumpy, hence his nickname!

A closet gay MP required that I obtain blonde, skinhead rent boys once a month. I was invited to his birthday party which was held in his boyfriend's luxury flat in Hampstead. The guests were all gay, including a female MP.

'Meet the Parliamentary dyke,' my host said. 'She's been dying to know if your tits are real or silicone.'

Much as I felt I could recognise a lesbian, this one took me by surprise, but being eager to add another MP to my list, I pulled up my blouse and invited her to examine my breasts. She fondled them in an erotic manner and I knew she fancied 'it'. After dinner, couples drifted off leaving us alone in the lounge. Things got very intimate and we ended up on the floor together.

The most unsavoury of these political prizes was 'Stinkbomb'. Although most men at that time ignored deodorants, or saw themn as a pansy practice, they managed to stay reasonably fresh with soap and water. 'Stinkbomb' could not; he was the utter end in hygiene. Under the Parliamentary appearance of a good suit were dirty armpits and scruffy underwear. He stank so much I was forced to incorporate a deodorant into a sex game. A flit-gun was filled with the most heavily perfumed one I could find and I'd aim it at him and scream: 'You filthy insect, you need spraying with my special insecticide.' And he'd be smothered in it. This worked out well because 'Stinkbomb' was also a submissive and liked domination.

Besides actual MPs, responses were coming in on the answering machine from professional men: lawyers, doctors and accountants with political connections. Stephen was keeping an eye on the sticker locations and renewed them as necessary whenever he popped into Parliament. My list of nicknames grew longer: 'Codseye the fisherman', 'Leonard the Lobbyist', 'Dolly Daydream the newscaster' and one who was christened 'Watersports' because his need was for me to urinate over his body while he masturbated.

My boyfriends recommended me to their friends and colleagues and before long I had to buy a new notebook so I could keep track of their likes and dislikes. I became a useful girl to take out to dinner if an MP was stuck in town for a late-night sitting. Some kept flats and houses where they stayed during the week. A few wives would travel up to the London addresses but if they didn't, there was a place for me. If they came to my flat, kept separate from 58 Eardley Crescent, it would be a romantic scenario. I had a strict rule, never to mix my boyfriends with clients. They came in all shapes and sizes, but a powerful position makes a man attractive, never ugly. All women like to know they are bedding someone who's affluent and influential. It makes them feel important and special. They could be with anyone, but they've chosen you.

Apart from buying dinner, these boyfriends were not obliged to pay any fee. If you trade sex for money, there's a barrier, and for my political ends, I didn't want this. By being 'user-friendly' (game to do anything), I received an incredible number of confidences and much information that would be extremely useful. When I got to know some of these men well, I confessed my true identity. They were amused at my double life and were of the unanimous opinion that I should challenge the Government's policy of taxing 'non-mercantile' prostitution. They encouraged me to stand up for my rights and suggested certain phrases which would make me sound more professional. My favourite was: 'Sexuality must be included on today's political agenda'. This was better than saying 'decriminalise prostitution' and sounded politically efficient.

I wondered if anyone would take me seriously but, as one of them said: 'If Emily Pankhurst had had that attitude, women would never have had the vote.' All of them encouraged me to stand up for what I believed in, and promised to help.

Having access to so many nice men left nothing for me to fantasise about myself, so I set myself some sexual challenges. I'd try to bed prominent people whom would rather die than be seen with a prostitute. The first one to endure my ceaseless flirting was Jeffrey Archer. Not because I particularly fancied him, but he had become a cult figure in the prostitution network after the *Daily Star* newspaper had named him as being involved in the Monica Coghlan scandal. In fact Mr Archer was later awarded substantial libel damages after showing the court that he had no involvement with Monica, but for a year I plagued him with kinky cards, all of which he ignored.

Then I set my targets higher, aiming for the leaders of the main political parties. Paddy Ashdown was the easiest to ambush because he had fewer minders round him. Lurking inside the House of Commons with other lobbyists, I went into 'ambush mode' the moment I saw him approaching the doorway. As he came 'in', I went 'out', engineering to accidentally-on-purpose bump smack into his chest.

'Whoops, at last we meet.' I grabbed his hand for a lingering shake. He pulled away and scurried off in horror. (This was long before he was given his 'Paddy Pantsdown' nickname.) As another ruse to get close to him, when the media asked who I considered to be Britain's sexiest man, I gave him the vote. Then I wormed my way into his clique by helping the Lib Dems at by-elections. I even sent in a membership fee to join, but someone leaked it to the Press, so I withdrew.

From the moment he headed his party, John Major proved impossible to get near. His minders were three deep. I tried lurking near his home, in Great Stukely, but the police chased me off.

My attempts to get near Neil Kinnock were rebuffed by his double-breasted mafia who pushed me out of the way with bully-boy tactics. The best I managed was a brief conversation with him outside the House of Commons when I organised a mass lobby on 14 October 1991 to legalise cannabis (another policy I'd taken on board). I asked whether or not he would legalise cannabis if he won office. He snapped four words: 'No, I'm against it.' His reply was to cost him General Election support of the Legalise Cannabis lobbies and pressure groups.

Personally I never use cannabis (or any other form of soft drug for that matter), but my hatred of bigotry found me taking on board other people's crusades. By studying various reports including that of Baroness Wootton (obtained from the House of Commons), I discovered that cannabis is a harmless herb, less addictive than nicotine and alcohol, drugs which are freely and legally available, and which kill thousands of people every year. Also, I was interested to learn that the hemp plant provides fuel, vegetable protein food, textiles and wood pulp; its easily grown crops can create massive employment and thus minimise third-world poverty and starvation.

During my serious study of politics I began to build up an arsenal of material with supporting statistics. One of my major stances was on the hypocrisy of government officials who publicly condemn prostitutes yet privately visit them. One classic example of this was a client I called the Witchfinder General who was ultimately responsible for the deregistration of my prostitution company, yet had the gall to visit me for business. I was so angry, I told him, 'I'll dance on your grave.' And I did! (There is something very satisfying about boogying on an 'enemy's' burial place in my highheeled boots.)

Another, much later, was the case of Sir Allan Green, the Director of Public Prosecutions, who was accused of kerb crawling at King's Cross. A street girl soliciting the same patch phoned me with the story half an hour after it happened, so by the time TV news, broadsheets, tabloids and radio phoned to 'break the scandal' and invite my comments, I already knew! What I really wanted to say was: 'Huh! Serves him right! Twice during his term of office I wrote begging him not to prosecute after I'd been busted on trumped-up charges. He ignored me!' But I kept my personal thoughts to myself and issued a press release:

> 'This is a classic example clearly demonstrating that besides the proverbial "dirty raincoat brigade", prominent men also require the outlet of sexual services. I therefore urge the DPP to use this example in a positive way by calling for legal brothels.'

However, he declined to promote new initiatives for prostitution, and melted into oblivion. I was aghast at this overt revelation of double standards: he broke a law on which the public faced prosecution, yet when caught with his own hand in the cookie jar he was let off.

Another of my major arguments was about the waste of taxpayers' money which was spent upholding archaic Victorian sex laws. Criminalising prostitutes was counter-productive because police, court and prison resources were depleted, and these resources could be better used on more positive things. Furthermore, although the enormous cost of abortions and curing sexually transmitted diseases was burdening the NHS, ironically the government drove prostitution underground. This made it difficult to provide safer sex education and health care to workers and clients, therefore pregnancy and disease were being encouraged to flourish! And, as sex education was not on the national curriculum, future prostitutes would therefore be sexually ignorant.

So many issues bugged me. There was a definite need for public police accountability, the only way to get rid of bent cops – and much corruption and fabricated evidence has now come to light in different parts of the country. The difficulty of getting legal aid also made me angry. If you were wronged, and were poor, there was little chance of redress. Extortionate legal fees prohibited you from getting justice. It was a case of 'Pay up – or shut up'.

Lack of government-funded scientific research into obesity was another issue that got my goat. Approximately 50 per cent of the population are overweight, yet the government give insignificant assistance to fatties. What with men on the moon, cloning and DNA, scientists should be able to make the calorie less fattening without any side effects! I reckon the Treasury is so happy raking in millions of pounds' taxation from expensive diet products that the government can't be bothered to change things.

Then there was the fact that when you die, your body belongs to the State. Unauthorised experiments are frequently carried out on bodies without even consulting their next of kin. I find this quite disgusting, and I'd never have believed it if two clients, a pathologist and a mortician, hadn't revealed secrets about their respective professions. Once when I went to meet the pathologist for business, he gave me a tour round his work place. 'Someone wanted a few scraps to make tests on,' he said, 'So I left them a pile of organs to choose from.' Then he scooped up a handful of leftover innards from a big mixed pile, put them inside a clear plastic bag and stuffed the bag inside a corpse with its torso sawn open. It was just like watching someone stuffing pre-packed giblets into a chicken. 'They're not even his *own* organs, but he's not going to worry!' he remarked.

And it's such a rigmarole if you want to be buried at sea! On every cruise I've been on, I've met sick elderly people who'd deliberately booked long trips in the hope of dying at sea, because they'd been denied access to this 'right' through normal channels. Quite frankly, I'd like an ocean burial myelf, rather than lie in some cemetery which in years to come gets sold off for ridiculously low money to greedy developers who dig up my bones and build an office block on the site.

I hated cruelty to animals, and felt strongly that our four-legged friends should be anaesthetised before carnivores slaughtered them. (My views eventually turned me vegetarian.) I passionately want blood sports and battery farming banned, and vivisection outlawed. Personally I thought experimentation would be better on humans – convicted murderers, for example, would make ideal specimens. They could pay their debt to society by being guinea pigs, and help science, technology and medicine. After all, humans can articulate how much substances sprayed in their eyes sting, or what side effects swallowing cosmetic ingredients have, and can do so much better than rabbits.

On the matter of fair play, I resented company bosses awarding themselves massive pay rises when their workers were being laid off.

Another thing I despised was the fact that ballot cards had counterfoil numbers on, so they weren't 'secret' ballots at all. The spooks at MI5 could look through them and know exactly how Joe Bloggs voted. There were *so* many things that needed to be challenged, and one by one they were festering inside me.

Having developed a close rapport with many MP clients and boyfriends, who all took me into their confidence, I soon realised that politics too was 'only a game'. Some of them were like overgrown schoolboys competing against each other for extra points. They were puppets on strings, with professional scriptwriters preparing their speeches, and few of them really cared about the issues raised by their constituents.

Every one of them was in awe of, and fantasised about, Margaret Thatcher. They loved the way 'Spitting Image' portrayed her, and saw her as the ultimate Dominatrix. Some even had me wearing a Maggie Thatcher mask during sex: 'Take this, you bitch!' 'Oh, Dennis! Oh, Dennis!' (Because I called my slaves 'Dennis' anyway, this game gave me an extra kick.) When one of Mrs Thatcher's old handbags was offered at auction, four Tory MP clients asked me to buy it so I could bash them over the head with it during kinky sex. They all gave me cash to bid for it (each thought he was the only one bidding for the bag, I never told them there were three rivals), but it was bought by a shopkeeper who paid over the odds because he wanted to promote his business by displaying the bag in his window.

This got me thinking. If men like this were running the country, I was sure I could do just as well, if not better. Perhaps the most significant thing they taught me was 'how to waffle on and wriggle out of answering questions'; they were all so good at that. The idea of standing for Parliament, and saying my fourpenny worth in the political arena, was now extremely appealing.

10

On the Hustings

For a long time I had been sounding out my colleagues and clients on the idea of forming a fringe political party. In 1988, from a significant number of reliable allies, I chose two women from the vice world and four subservient slaves to join me as the party's nerve centre – the decision makers.

Our dedication earned us the name of 'The Magnificent Seven'. We gave ourselves NEC (National Executive Committee) positions with responsibilities for particular tasks. Samuel, an accountant, was our costing expert; Stephen, a lawyer, was our legal adviser and campaign co-ordinator; David, a library attendant (useful for specialist books and press clippings), was our media liaison officer; Leslie, a truck driver, became head of transportation; Marilyn, a prostitute, became our policy researcher; Rebecca, a prostitute's maid, became our secretary; and I was voted leader. I also became treasurer because I held the purse strings, and subsidised the party from my immoral earnings.

We devised our 'constitution' (the rules of the party), and formulated our policies which took three weeks of intensive discussions and a few heated arguments. As we were a democratic party, majority votes were required before policies could be accepted on to our manifesto. There were quite a few policies proposed by others which I was undecided about at that time – for example, 'troops out of Ireland' – so I abstained from voting. Eventually we had over a hundred policies, all with valid justification to back up new legislation.

The next step was to christen the party. I suggested the name 'corrective' – 'to correct the entire system with radical reforms and new ideas'. Everyone loved it! We wanted an original catchphrase or motto, so I went to Waterstone's bookshop and looked up the word 'corrective' in every dictionary. The Hugo and Oxford were the best, defining 'corrective' as 'putting right' and 'counteracting anything wrong or harmful'.

For cost efficiency, we squeezed two A5 leaflets from a regular A4 sheet of paper, but unfortunately they were too small to include the whole of our manifesto: there was only room for fifty policies, even with the smallest legible print. Therefore, we selected fifty issues which we considered most important as our 'Statement of Policies'. We all liked pink, gay members in particular thinking it 'camp', so pink was voted the party colour. Stationery, rosettes and T-shirts were ordered in the relevant hue.

During the following year we recruited into our party as many friends, neighbours, work-mates, and clients as possible, as well as anyone else who was interested. Membership subscription was £15 with a reduced rate of £5 for the unwaged. In some cases, unwaged activists' subscriptions were waived altogether; they were worth their weight in gold just for their enthusiasm and ability to canvass the electorate.

We didn't notify the media of our existence until Sir Leon Brittan vacated his seat in Richmond, Yorkshire, which caused a by-election in February 1989. Other Corrective Party members were too shy to stand for election, so this was my opportunity to try my political wings. I discovered that my MPs and political friends who had been so big on encouragement at the beginning, now became small on support. The costs of going it alone were prohibitive and somewhat worrying. I needed £500 for the deposit, and at least a couple of grand for election leaflets, hotels and general expenses.

Therefore, when a newspaper offered to sponsor me, I accepted. I knew they'd expect a 'Miss Whiplash' story with me dressed in obligatory leathers, boots and whip, but getting started was most important. Unfortunately, I didn't realise the extent to which they would trivialise my serious message, and this took me two years to live down.

Accompanied by Molly (another prostitute) and several slaves, I travelled by train to Darlington. En route, Molly and I both picked up punters in the bar and serviced them in the toilets. On arrival, a journalist called Jimmy and his photographer met us from the train

CORRECTIVE PARTY STATEMENT OF POLICIES

1. Liberalize censorship laws on pornographic material.
2. Decrease the black economy by legalizing prostitution.
3. Fund insufficient health, education and welfare services from currently wasted revenue sources, e.g.; mercantile sexual services.
4. NHS sexual services should be available for people who are mentally ill or disabled.
5. Equalize the age of consent for homosexuals and heterosexuals.
6. Abolish section 28 and clause 25.
7. End homophobia in the British Armed Forces.
8. Free condoms to all, including men in prison.
9. Keep the state out of our bedrooms – Free the Operation Spanner victims.
10. Pre-puberty sex education on the national curriculum.
11. Annual Parliamentary elections for political accountability.
12. Freedom of Information – governmental secrets are a bad habit.
13. Ensure secret ballots – end electoral numbering of counterfoils.
14. Cancel third world debts.
15. More care and resources to integrate the mentally ill into society.
16. Government sponsorship for housing, transport and infrastructure.
17. Government national bank for fixed rate mortgages.
18. Ban vivisection. Experiment only on human volunteers.
19. Anaesthetics must be used before animal slaughter.
20. Outlaw blood sports. Appoint State professionls to curb 'pests'.
21. More incentives for free range eggs to phase out battery farming.
22. Widen adoption availability for heterosexuals and homosexuals.
23. A 35 hour working week.
24. An equal European wage and pension.
25. Speedy European integration on the right terms.
26. Improve pollution controls of rivers, sea, air and land.
27. Ban unnecessary wasteful wrappings and packaging on goods.
28. A Ministry of Women to promote gender equality.
29. Widen criminal and civil legal aid availability and jury service.
30. Public accountability of the police to prevent brutality and corruption.
31. Legalize anti-rape noxious gas sprays to protect women.
32. More scientific research into obesity, calories and metabolisms.
33. More scientific research into solar, water, wind and coal energy.
34. Legalize paid surrogate mothers.
35. Permit Sunday trading with the proviso of volunteer staff.
36. Tax the Monarch's private wealth and profits.
37. Legalize voluntary euthanasia.
38. Appoint child ombudspersons – this is the only way to eliminate child abuse.
39. Food subsidies must relate to domestic needs not surplus for export.
40. Protect our open spaces, countryside, hedgerows and wild life.
41. More public information on pharmaceuticals and pesticides.
42. Legalize cannabis – cannabis is less harmful than nicotine.
43. Cut warfare to pay for welfare – world nuclear disarmament.
44. Proportional Representation.
45. MPs must delare their entire business interests.
46. Better consumer rights and means of redress.
47. Better burials rights, e.g.; at sea, or on private land.
48. Ban unnecessary medical experiments on corpses without consent of next of kin.
49. Percentage pay rises of employers must equal those of employees.
50. Outlaw discrimination on minorities and stereotypes.

and drove us to our smart hotel. My room was a few doors from a rival candidate, and I made plans to accost him in the night – easy peasy! In the meantime, Jimmy arranged a public meeting where he announced that my 50-point manifesto matched my 50 inch bust. He hired an election van and gave me £100 to decorate it: this I spent on black stockings, bras and panties which were festooned from the roof rack.

The rival candidates tried upstaging me with catty remarks like: 'She might know everything about sex, but she's a virgin to politics'! I hit back by publicly addressing the Tory candidate (William Hague, MP) as 'Little Willie', with emphasis on the 'little', and uttering innuendos like: 'I'll thrash the Tories black and blue'; and 'Politicians need more discipline.'

The town was buzzing with male activists drafted in to help their respective parties. I couldn't resist flirting with them all, even managing to persuade some candidates to pose for saucy photos. No-one escaped our propositons for kinky threesomes, not even the police or the mayor. Daily (and nightly) we gathered new recruits, promising free sex to everyone who voted Corrective. However, our frolics came to an unexpected end when the photographer got drunk and kept pestering me. I didn't think it funny. This resulted in my sponsor and me falling out, and my political credibility was ruined before it even began. However, in spite of this farce I polled 116 votes, which showed that some people seemed willing to support me on entertainment value alone.

Back at Eardley Crescent, my business interests had been neglected. The proofs for a series of kinky massage ads to run in local London papers had not been carefully checked. To my astonishment, I had a phone call from a Sister at St Mary's Covent in South Kensington. A stream of calls was coming in from men who thought they were about to receive the ultimate thrill of bedding a nun. It appeared our numbers were different by only one digit; the Convent's had been printed in the paper. I couldn't apologise enough, but she reassured me that she could handle the situation as she was an ex social worker. My greater concern was that she would be shocked with what was being said. I was annoyed that those thick men would actually believe a convent was the front for a knocking shop. Some randy men wouldn't take no for an answer until I stationed one of my minders outside. When he caught a punter offering money to a nun in the street, he blacked his eyes, and the message went out. The convent was left alone from then on.

Having sorted that out, I retreated to a health farm just outside London, in an attempt to rejuvenate myself. It was important that I be close enough to pop back to Earl's Court to deal with Corrective Party matters. Since buying the Lordship of Laxton Manor, I had taken the title of Lady Laxton, and booked in as such. During after-dinner conversation, the subject of politics arose and mention was made of a by-election in the Vale of Glamorgan. I was immediately alert; here was my chance to embark on a proper campaign.

As the sponsoring newspaper had done the ground-work the first time, I wasn't aware of the drill until I telephoned the Returning Officer in Barry next morning. I discovered there was only one day left before the close of nominations. If I was going to stand as a candidate, I had to get there fast. I temporarily abandoned my health programme. My Rolls had suffered so much malicious damage, I had given it up for a Range Rover which would be a much more suitable political wagon. I charged off down the M4 to Barry, a hick town at the back of beyond, suffering from limited accommodation, most of which had already been taken by the main parties.

Eventually I found a three-star hotel near the seafront which was being renovated. The entry to the parking lot was uphill and arched with scaffolding, but there was no warning of limited height access. The car and I made it through, but the brand-new roof-rack did not! The crash against the scaffolding brought people running from the bar, one of whom was a local builder. As he got me out, I quickly hired him to make the pink political placards I needed to fit round the front and sides of the Range Rover.

The manager of the hotel made it quite clear that he resented my persona and all that I stood for. During my stay I had to make several complaints to the manager, which culminated in a later argument over the bill. There was a fault on their telephone monitoring system and I was charged for calls I hadn't made. I expected my bill to be adjusted and left without paying.

In the meantime, I hired a cab to get me about. The driver declared himself a fan, and helped me to get the ten local signatures needed on my nomination papers before being officially accepted. He warned me that as Barry was a staunch Labour stronghold,

Corrective Party support would not be easy to find. He was willing to save me the time of going through the electoral rolls by driving me round to members of his family. He was sure they would provide the necessary signatures, and they did. I was then able to return to the Civic Office, pay my £500 deposit, and be declared an official candidate.

When I returned to the health farm, there were some strange looks at the pink placards and posters adorning my Range Rover in the car park. During the three weeks before polling day, I began a very hectic life, alternating between Barry and the health farm, three days here and three days there. I was paying a lot of money for my suite, but since it was the only one in the place, I didn't want to risk losing it if I vacated. This meant paying twice – for the Barry hotel and for the suite.

The massage staff noticed I was missing from my treatments, but they read an article in the *Daily Mirror* that week with a photo and headlines: 'Miss Whiplash Expecting a Whippersnapper. The Dad's an MP!' The article then went on to discuss me standing in the Vale of Glamorgan by-election. Guests and staff began to question me on Corrective Party policies.

During my campaign I had managed to organise a crew of helpers; they included a prostitute's maid who preferred to be called a 'receptionist'; Philip, a gay boy who occasionally helped me out with stickers around London; and Mike, his boyfriend, who happened to live in a neighbouring village. We canvassed the town, experiencing a lot of abuse from kids, who stood in gangs on street corners, chanting 'Labour! Labour!' and throwing stones at my election wagon as we drove by. The local police exhibited a similar hostility; through the loud-hailers newly mounted on the roof rack, I was saying, 'Police accountablity. End police brutality.' This ruffled their feathers somewhat.

Undaunted, we carried leaflets over the fields to farm workers, down country lanes to catch cowmen moving the herds for milking, and I personally knocked on the door of every cottage I saw. After this determined effort, it was dismaying to see the *South Wales Echo* sending us up: they published a carton showing a naked man with a rosette on his genitals labelling him a member of the Corrective Party.

To counteract this trivialisation, I placed an ad in a sister paper, the *Western Mail*: 'Contrary to the image being displayed by the

"He can't be Jehovah's Witness — they come in pairs. He can't be replacement windows or he'd have a brief case — he's gotta be the Corrective Party"

local press and television, I do stand for some highly important issues to which every voter should address themselves.' I could only afford the space to list a few policies I thought the local people might be sympathetic to.

It was frustrating that, however much I tried, I could not get anyone to take me seriously. A television crew broadcast my 'out-takes' instead of my carefully prepared campaign speech. The Barry Lions Club (a charitable organisation) invited me to talk to them at a dinner about my manifesto, but I discovered that what they really wanted was 'tits and bums' entertainment. I obliged by recounting my most kinky sexual experiences. This did nothing to enhance the sensible political image I was trying to portray.

My spirits were lifted by the news that Jeffrey Archer was in the nearby market town, Cowbridge, to support the Tory candidate. I made up my mind that he would not be able to avoid me. With the help of a friendly television crew in on the plan (they were staying at my hotel), I played the frumpy housewife, hair pulled back, half glasses perched on my nose. My aim was to ambush Archer and confront him with the irresponsible Tory attitude towards prostitution. He came on scene in his element, accompanied by the Tory candidate and an aide with a loud-hailer trying to pull in the crowds. He was sure he was going to make some admiring little housewife's day when he grabbed me by the hand.

'Good afternoon, my dear, how are you today?'

Tracked by television, I went in for the kill: 'I'm Lindi St Clair of the Corrective Party. What are you Tories going to do to clean up the streets . . .?'

It was my intention to continue on the subject of kerb-crawling, but the candidate jumped in. 'We're taking steps to clean up the streets by authorising more garbage wagons.'

What a twit! The crowd knew full well that I was referring to sex, not litter. Best of all, the Corrective Party had their moment on Channel 4 News.

On voting day, in a last-ditch effort to gather support for my party, I drove to every polling station in and out of the town. The police seized the opportunity to tell me off for frightening the livestock with my loud-hailer.

Game to the last, I stayed on for the count. It was a disappointing result. Only thirty-five votes.

I was beginning to question whether politics was worth all the aggravation I had suffered. I had canvassed to the point of exhaustion and been humiliated into the bargain. It was Marilyn, the Green Party candidate, who consoled me. She said it had taken them ten years to make sense to the electorate about the ozone layer. She was also the only one to inform me that candidates were entitled to free postings of leaflets to the entire constituency. (This usually costs approximately £7,000, the number of constituents times postage.) Her words encouraged me to keep on trying.

When the election was over, I checked out of the health club, a stone lighter and 2 inches less around the boobs, and started plotting for the European election in June 1989. By contesting a London seat, I would be on home territory. This would save on accommodation, and that in turn would allow more funds for election material, something that had been in short supply in Barry. I needed thirty signatures this time for the nomination form, and these were collected by two friends who canvassed their pals in pubs. I was also able to enlist punters to leaflet the constituency, and some of my submissive slaves went happily round with sandwich boards publicising the Party. A big pink placard went up on the outside wall at Eardley Crescent to display the Corrective Party motto, and I made space for a public meeting on the premises above the dungeons.

When I announced the date, and invited the media, I made it quite clear I would tape their interviews and the meeting itself, and would not tolerate any misquotes or misrepresentation. Denied the chance of any silly, sensationalist scoop, they were not interested in my public meeting, hence only one journalist turned up. But colleagues and friends from the sex and gay scene were there to support me: they included a hospital health worker, a doctor, a Tory activist, a City businessman, a writer and the editor of *Penthouse* magazine.

Later, sixty-three members of the public arrived; fourteen of them joined and paid their £15 membership subscription. I accept that curiosity probably played its part, but the genuineness of my campaign appeared to win their support. I was to gain more followers at a party thrown by Helen Buckingham (the prostitute made bankrupt by the taxman). Her guest of honour was Delores French – an American prostitute – in town to promote her autobiography on the Terry Wogan show. She agreed to canvass with me in Soho. We drove round in the Range Rover calling for a repeal of the sex laws through the loud-hailers.

My canvassing for the European election was sabotaged by the Barry police, still resentful of my intrusion on their patch. They were making a case of the hotel bill, still in dispute. One of my friends at the Met tried to intercede on my behalf by assuring them I was honourable and would settle at a civil court. They were not satisfied with this, their aim was to 'get' me. The cops hammered on my door every two hours throughout the night. I turned out the lights, ignored the phones, and sat in the dark, plotting my next move. The answering machine clicked, with a message from the local bobby who was a right busybody: 'We know you're in there. If you don't come to the station voluntarily, we will nick you while you are electioneering which would be a bit embarrassing – and you wouldn't want that, would you!'

My dispute was not criminal, and so the police had no business poking their noses in. The following afternoon, I telephoned Kensington police station, offering to come in to explain the situation on condition I wasn't arrested, because this was clearly a civil matter. The bastards double-crossed me. They detained me until the Barry police came to collect me at midnight. One of the officers, a little Hitler, said 'You're nothing but a London tart, we don't want your sort in Barry.' He handcuffed me – over-zealous to say the least – and then they drove me at high speed to South Wales where I was kept in custody until give bail.

This did not prove the end of my difficulties. Although I'd explained that I had to be in London on 6 June for the Euro election, the charge sheet was made up for me to surrender bail that very day. They had me in tears before I could convince them to change it.

My absence from London caused me to miss several important newspaper, radio and television interviews. I did as much as I could with the little time left and arrived at the count with my supporters ready to cheer the results. My campaign co-ordinator suggested that I work out a speech, incorporating concern over AIDS. There were already some shocking statistics. I hoped this would bring home an important point of my manifesto: if prostitution were regulated, the spread of HIV could be minimised.

I polled 707 votes. The only spoiler present was one of my rival fringe candidates who attempted to upstage me and interrupted my speech. I was still too new at this game to react effectively, but each such encounter taught me more about how I could. He might try again, but he would never succeed. The new Labour MEP, Stan Newens, admitted he agreed with one of the other points of my manifesto – the one relating to consenting adults and homosexuality – and he suggested we meet for a discussion at his office. This made me feel I had achieved a major breakthrough.

I now had to return to Barry for the court case. Everyone seemed to have painted a false picture of what had happened there. I might have been new to politics, but not to courts, and I had a barrister, Tim Sewell, to represent me. The trial took four days but the jury took only ten minutes to decide I was innocent of all charges. I was acquitted. (I was entitled to costs of £2,000, but I never got them.)

Constant innuendo during the European campaign made me consider changing the Party name. We voted to change it to the National Independent Correct Edification party. This had the acronym of NICE. I changed my own name to Lindi Love so that we could take it even further by using the slogan 'All You Need is Love'. The new literature had a picture of me in a dark suit, with the House of Commons in the background.

The new Party name was tried out at the next by-election I fought, one in Mid Staffordshire. I hired a light aircraft to tow a banner saying 'BE NICE – VOTE LOVE' to attract more potential voters. Everything was going well. We were a large enough team to split up in different directions and canvass the constituency. Then, the Returning Officer, who has the last say in all elections, declared my leaflets invalid because they lacked the mandatory statement: 'Printed and published by. . . .' (This rather expensive hiccup was another part of my political learning process.) My only way of reaching the electorate was through an invitation from the local Press to submit a 250-word letter outlining policies. It wasn't enough, the vote was a pathetic fifty-nine. I concluded I'd 'done a David Owen' – made a mistake in changing the name of my party. No-one knew what NICE was all about whereas people were well aware of what the Corrective Party stood for.

Back in 'Corrective' mode, I decided to capitalise on the popularity of the name 'Miss Whiplash' (with randy men, kinks and voters sympathetic to the cause), and that was how I went into the next campaign, at Knowsley South, in the Liverpool area. It was here that I discovered that the Post Office stipulate leaflets must be folded to a particular size to qualify for the free-drop. As printers charge a penny per fold, this adds an extra £500 per 50,000 leaflets on top of the initial outlay for printing and artwork (prohibitive rules to discourage fringe candidates with low budgets). Also, commuting back and forth to London to keep my various business and personal commitments going – very necessary to fund my political ambitions – proved very tiring and expensive. The chance to do a radio interview with the other candidates didn't turn out as I'd hoped. The Labour man was so obnoxiously confident he would win, he more or less took over. For all of that, I polled ninety-nine votes – a 200 per cent increase on the previous election.

Even after weighing up the cost and effort, I couldn't resist the opportunity to contest by-elections as they came along. Each was a different kind of challenge and expanded my experience and political credibility. When Eastbourne came up, I thought the fact it was reasonably close to home made it worthwhile, especially as once more I could cut down on accommodation expenses. We found a central location for campaign headquarters, press-released the manifesto, and the crew and I set out to leaflet the town. Since the area was full of old people, we were constantly asked what we could offer them. Our response was that it was in everybody's interest to amend the sex laws before we all died of AIDS.

This did not deter the local newspaper from publishing a derogatory and intimidating article which was headlined: 'Get out of town, Miss Whiplash, we don't want you.' It printed the opinions of the other candidates and of the Council of Churches. They claimed I had no right to bring what they called 'a vaudeville campaign' into the town and desecrate the seat of Ian Gow who had been so tragically blown up.

I examined the Representation of the People Act minutely. My critics were in the wrong. It was a crime for anyone to put undue pressure on the electorate to vote otherwise. Nor could one make a mis-statement about a candidate: I had never been a vaudeville performer! Now totally sure of my position, I insisted that the Returning Officer take action. This had them all in a flap. I was the first person ever to exercise this right, which meant bringing in the police to lay a formal charge. My complaint was not upheld, which surprised me as there was ample evidence, but I suppose, since I was Miss Whiplash, the system and its bureaucrats felt able to ignore my rights. (Interestingly enough, in April 1992, the Conservative candidate for Copeland was to follow suit. After the General Election he claimed a breach of Section 75 of the Representation of the People Act in relation to British Nuclear Fuel's apparent support for Jack Cunningham, Labour.)

The final result of the Eastbourne vote was 216 for me, excellent considering the odds. It broke down to 10 per cent of the Labour vote and 50 per cent of the Greens. Since this was still only October 1990, and I had only started in earnest in February 1989, I was the only party that could claim a 500 per cent increase in such a short time!

I felt well into my stride as I entered the by-election in Ribble Valley in Lancashire, in March 1991. The fact that it was a staunch Tory seat in a rural area didn't bother me. I was told: 'They won't be interested in sex up here.'

Decriminalising prostitution was an asset to everyone; besides which, this was not the only item on my manifesto. I had learned to be very adept at examining local issues, and by now had a policy of sending for back-dated copies of the local papers so that I knew exactly what made an area tick. For Ribble Valley I had swotted up on farming and pesticides, and various issues the other candidates were promoting. The Tory candidate, Nigel Evans, was known for his views on the restoration of capital punishment, so I nicknamed him 'Nigel the Noose' and urged the electorate to reject his view on hanging. My cleverly worded Press release set the entire Ribble Valley constituency talking:

> 'New legislation is often tried on a sample population; for instance, the poll tax was first tested in Scotland. Therefore, the Corrective Party suggests that legislation on hanging be applied to a sample population also, preferably a willing one. Members of Parliament have shown such willingness and thus make an ideal sample, upon criteria, for instance, of failing to properly declare their business interests, and arms trading with Iraq.'

Some of the Liberal Democrat activists were by now old friends. We accompanied each other on poster-board patrol (in the dead of night). During this campaign I was summoned to court in London for non-payment of poll tax. In support of the millions who couldn't afford it, I refused to pay mine. Word got out, and I held court daily in the Ribble Valley pub which I'd made my HQ, and hordes of people came to seek poll tax advice. Monitoring my competition, I attended all the public meetings held by the Tories and Socialists. At one, Michael Heseltine recognised me and blatantly refused to take my question from the floor. Therefore I heckled him and gave him a volley of abuse as he left. He never rose to the bait.

However, back at the pub, local men were queueing up to consult me on various, rather more basic, matters. One shyly requested some advice on how to diminish the size of his giant penis. This was too much of a challenge for a sexual enthusiast like myself. I nicknamed him 'Heathcliff', and he became my sex slave. He took me sightseeing to the ruins of Clitheroe Castle, built in 1186. The views from there were breathtaking: the green valley below was surrounded by mysterious hills steeped in mystery and witchcraft. It was the perfect place to fulfil a long-standing fetish: to make love in a real medieval dungeon with a rugged, tall, dark stranger.

This interlude did not distract me from my real reasons for being in the area. I had a Press call outside the Conservative Club. Wearing a mortar-board and gown, and carrying a cane taken from the House of Fetish and Fantasy, I chalked the most important points of my campaign on a blackboard (loaned by the local Red Cross office).

CORRECTIVE POLICIES

A AXE POLL TAX
Don't pay it!
B BETTER SERVICES
C CUT POLLUTION
D DEFEND NHS
E END WAR IN THE GULF & IRELAND
F FIGHT SEXUAL TABOOS

VOTE ST CLAIR

This campaign was at the time of the Gulf war. I received hundreds of letters from lonely, frustrated servicemen who got my address from a tabloid newspaper. Although I'm against war, and politically felt that our soldiers were used as cannon fodder, I did my bit to help keep up morale. On my word processor I wrote out various kinky sex letters, then ran them off in bulk, and posted them off to the British Forces' mail box. 'Blueys' (blue airmail letters) arrived by the post bag as squaddies, air and naval crew passed my address to their mates. Every serviceman said the same thing, how horny he felt, and how painful it was getting sand under his foreskin as he wanked off. I developed quite a friendship with those boys and to make their private hours a little more pleasurable I sent out quite a few videos and explicit photos. I even had special 'Tickets to Ride' (free brothel passes) printed as stickers in desert camouflage colours; these were stuck on tanks, planes, guns and kitbags. Occasionally those who had the time and opportunity called me for telephone sex whereby they relieved themselves as I spoke dirty.

Back in the Ribble Valley, an invitation to Clitheroe Royal Grammar School was my first opportunity to get my message across to students. I was warned that there had been a poor turnout for every other candidate, but for me it was a packed house, and they were an enthusiastic audience (though inclined to laugh at the slightest hint of innuendo). The fact that the talk went over time from fifteen minutes to forty was flattering, and afterwards I was mobbed for souvenirs and autographs. I felt I had taken a step forward in my political career. These young people were my votes for the future.

The election count was held at Stoneyhurst, a Roman Catholic college with beautiful stone-mullioned windows. I bumped into a politico who had been nasty to me at Michael Heseltine's meeting.

He grabbed my hand in a 'come-to-bed' shake, and chatted me up. Usually I'm sexually available to any and every political person, but there were better fish to fry in the shape of eager 'toyboys' from the college, sons of men of power, who represented future clients and sources of information. I have always believed in planning ahead! I spent two hours autographing the inside covers of their textbooks, and collecting their telephone numbers for my 'young-drawer' file.

The Conservatives were so confident they were going to win, they stayed in an exclusive huddle in one corner. I chose to be with the Lib Dems in the opposite corner. The atmosphere was electric, as if a major boxing championship was about to commence. And there was indeed to be a surprise knockout – the Lib Dems won. Looking back now, from the vantage point of the General Election results, the Conservatives were due the last laugh. 'Nigel the Noose' got in.

I had a few more elections to go before that, including Monmouth – where I was again forced to exercise my rights under the Representation of the People Act – Langbaurgh and Hemsworth. At Mommouth the local television station proposed to leave me out of a studio debate which was supposed to be between all the candidates contesting the seat. It was all or nothing as far as I was concerned, and I protested. Rather than include me, the debate was cancelled. The Atticus column in the *Sunday Times* summed up neatly what had happened: 'TSW found itself outspanked by Miss Whiplash, the Corrective Party's candidate.'

All those by-elections had taken place in less than two years. Although incredibly hard work each and every attempt to gain a seat had been a revelation. I gained confidence and I learned an enormous amount about political procedures. I'd also seen the adoption of Corrective Party policies. We had campaigned for the televising of the proceedings of the House of Commons, for instance; and I believe it was largely due to our non-stop campaigning that 'rape in marriage' was recognised in law. As an *Independent* editorial remarked in June 1991:

'It is an honourable part of the British political tradition that the big parties should filch ideas from their less inhibited rivals.'

The piece went on to list my arguments for legalising brothels and finished by saying 'She is right on all counts.'

During the by-elections, I also extended the list of MPs with whom I was sexually acquainted. In my travels to the various constituencies, I bribed the management to put me in rooms close to those of visiting MPs of all political persuasions. Few could resist my open-door policy, especially if I waited there at night in a black fishnet body stocking and stilettos!

Despite mixing business, pleasure and politics, the Corrective Party is not a self-indulgent hobby. I feel I can represent the people. I've 'been there', suffered some of the same problems with housing, the health service and the police. I was now so politically motivated, that instead of counting men as customers, they had become potential voters. However, the main purpose of the by-elections had been to provide me with a springboard into the General Election. That was going to cost a great deal of money. The by-elections' costs were pushing £20,000, and although donations had come in, they were nothing compared to the millions the major parties received. If I was going to field fifty candidates to qualify for a Party Political broadcast, the Party needed even more funding and supporters.

Conservative, Labour and Liberal Democrat manifestos always excluded prostitution, so in order to force the issue on 'Moral John', 'Joker Neil' and 'Smooth Dude' (my nicknames for the then party leaders), I speculated £2,000 of Corrective Party funds on a solace front-page advert in a major broadsheet newspaper, the *Independent*. I'd spent weeks designing a specific ad which would deliberately get up John Major's nose; I wanted the topic to bounce across every mainstream political dinner-table. I also expected my cheek to score points with sympathetic MPs and radicals.

However, I could not have envisaged the enormous amount of international media attention my actions would attract. From 7.30 that morning – 17 June 1991 – I was inundated with hacks wanting exclusive copy. My six telephones rang their bells off, and camera crews were camped on my front porch, even calling through the letter box as I ate my branflakes.

My controversial ad was headed 'PROSTITUTION' in large bold print, a title guaranteed to gain the attention of both supporters and opposers. There were two cut-out coupons: one was an application to join the Party; the other, an open letter to the Prime Minister asking him to call for legal brothels, with the explanation that driving prostitution underground into a furtive, stigmatised and illegal environment opened the flood-gates to organised crime, and encouraged disease, danger and death. At the bottom of the coupon was a blank space reserved for those in favour to sign their names before sending it off to Number 10 Downing Street, London SW1.

For days I smugly chortled, envisaging thousands of coupons arriving on John Major's desk, swamping his in-tray. Even if they went straight into his dustbin, I knew it would still 'rattle his cage'! But I felt fully justified publicly expressing the views of Britain's prostitutes, clients and a significant number of broad-minded adults.

For several weeks afterwards, membership applications flooded into the Corrective Party headquarters. Two thousand, four hundred and sixty-one new members – of which only 5 per cent were female – joined up, from places as far-flung as Thurso and Penzance. And most positive of all was the previously unavailable opportunity to spread the Corrective word across the world via twenty-seven media interviews for Brazil, Canada, South Africa, Australia, Spain, Italy, Germany, Finland, Portugal, Hungary, Sweden, Norway, and even Russia. It appeared the Corrective boat had finally come in!

Of course there were time-wasters – 309 to be exact – each of whom donated minuscule sums like one or two pence. They used silly names like Mr Wan King (wanking) and Mr Hugh Jardon (huge hard-on), and wrote sexually explicit notes. Until then, I would never have believed so many half-brained goons read the quality press. This was the response I expected from gutter-press ads, which I'd purposely avoided. But to make a positive out of a negative, I've kept the letters, and one day I'll publish them!

'Moral John' lived up to my expectations and totally ignored my efforts to promote public awareness of today's inadequate sex laws. In fact, out of countless letters I've addressed to him since he took office, none have been acknowledged, let alone received the dignity of a reply. Yet surprisingly enough, his predecessor – the former occupant of Number 10, Margaret Thatcher – always managed to muster some response, even if it was a standard rebuffing 'one liner' ('thank you for your letter, the contents of which we note'), from her secretary.

On the whole, my ad certainly set tongues wagging, both for and against, and I was particularly amused when one moralist with an overactive mind had the gall to complain to the Advertising Standards Association that my ad was offensive. Naturally the ASA rejected this bigoted suggestion.

After three months, the burst of support began to dwindle down to only a few daily inquiries, and it occurred to me there were millions of clandestine male supporters, who would love to help my campaign, but feared committing themselves in writing. With this theory in mind, I placed a follow-up front-page advert on 25 November 1991. But this time, I included the 'magic words' which ensured total discretion. The coupon said:

'Oh dear, I'm grey, but I want to secretly help your campaign on a non-membership basis. I enclose a donation of. . .
My pseudonym is. . . . *My box number is* . . . .'

As anticipated, many supporters were forthcoming. A total of 12,324 'closet Correctives' were flushed out from 'Greysville' (an imaginary place where routine, stereotypical grey men dwell). Amongst the most interesting 'coups' were two members of the judiciary, from Middle Temple and Lincoln's Inn, a man who worked at the Royal Mint, the editor of a religious newspaper, and a popular television game-show host. An avalanche of letters arrived enclosing postal orders, and cash donations came by recorded delivery (not surprisingly there weren't any identifying cheques). Some men donated their political and legal expertise; others offered their skills and services like printing, speech writing and transportation. What took the biggest burden from my shoulders were willing pen-pushers who happily handled the non-stop mail which was gradually snowing me under.

My political profile was rapidly growing, but there were always 'Doubting Thomases' ready to scoff at my expectations. To them I proudly said: 'There are new soldiers in the political trenches, and they're called Correctives!' They had no answer to this!

Despite all this excitement, in the event I didn't have enough time to organise my forces, and decided it would be better to sit this General Election out and come in with strength next time. A.N. Wilson in the London *Evening Standard* said my withdrawal was a loss, because the Corrective Party was the only one not committed to making the voters' lives a misery!

11

The Other Side of Sex

When I started my electioneering, it became a non-stop obsession, which found me neglecting my House of Fetish and Fantasy. Thus I lost 95 per cent of my income, plus a significant amount of impatient clients; they defected to other Mistresses whom they considered 'more reliable timekeepers'. A few grizzly old MPs who themselves were frequently absent from Parliament had sarcastically snapped that my attendance record was as bad as theirs! But I didn't care, my thirst for political action became my priority. Naturally, this caused my 'petty cash' to dry up, so in order to continue living in the manner to which I was accustomed, as well as campaigning, I spent a few days devising alternative ways of making cash, based on what I knew best – kinky sex.

To accommodate the running of new businesses I registered two companies – 'Slutco UK Ltd' and 'Rent-A-Fantasy Ltd'. I thought it an absolute cheek that the registrar of Companies House refused to accept my registrations unless I wrote him a letter promising not to trade in prostitution. He totally dismissed the fact that the High Court and House of Lords had declared prostitution a taxable 'trade'! I further fancied adding the name 'Whiplash Ltd' to my empire, and was astonished to find this title already registered by two men in the Midlands. I wrote offering to buy their company name, but they didn't reply.

Drawing on my sexual experiences, with the intention of enticing the debauched male (I reckon there are about 12 million of them in Britain), I created 'Castle Doom', a fictitious, impenetrable lair in the middle of nowhere, where twenty-five kinky Mistresses with names like 'Stiletto Hellcat' and 'Bizarre Babe' ruled supreme over their sex slaves. (The men actually believed it existed!) I prepared text and artwork, then published my 'Castle Doom Bible' which contained deviant sex stories, erotic drawings and kinky competitions, like submitting poems on 'Why they deserve to be caned'. The best entry won a free discipline session, and the thousands of entries gave me ample material for later publications. In order to avoid the huge advertising costs involved in launching this project, I did a deal with a newspaper, and permitted them to publish photographs of myself with two actors from the cast of 'East Enders' whom I'd met at a party. In return I received free classified ad space. My 'bibles' sold like hot cakes. Reprints of 1,000 a time sold out within weeks.

I was keen to maximise income in order to fund future election campaigns, so the next step up my business ladder was to launch 'Castle Doom' 0898 sex lines. I didn't want chat lines whereby callers talk one to one with live girls: massive insurance premiums were required by watchdog committees which went into a special fund set up to compensate callers tricked into hanging on the line and running up enormous bills. I chose to run 'pre-recorded' tapes (known as Adult Services) managed by BT in return for a commission of approximately 50 per cent of the revenue generated. Callers listened to kinky dialogue and sound effects relayed from digital computers. BT vetted the tapes for swear words or phrases they considered obscene or indecent, and at first they banned my material which contained dialogue like 'You've messed your pants' or 'What's all that sticky stuff?' They claimed it was too explicit! I disagreed and felt it was a con for callers to pay premium rates of 25p plus (48p now) per minute to listen to 'non-adult twaddle'! You either had *adult* services or you didn't!

The only way to transmit 'value for money' innuendoes (not obscene, but clever, erotic double entendres) was to buy my own independent computer equipment, install fifty or more telephone lines and pay through the nose for 'service contracts' (in case the equipment broke down). This meant capital outlay of £160,000 which I didn't have. BT suggested I try an 'audio text' bureau (companies who rent out space on independent systems in return for a small rent, and who are less fussy about tape contents). BT recommended two such bureaux: International Telecom PLC and its sister company Voice Systems International Ltd. I took BT's advice, approached them both and signed a contract. After buying recording equipment and mixing decks to make the tapes, my bank accounts went into the red. In order to get started, I had to borrow £15,000 from my friendly bank manager and spent a lot on an elaborate promotion campaign. My artistic flair came in handy in designing an enticing display ad, listing forty-eight numbers for 'Castle Doom's' Mistresses, a number of 'Lindi St Clair's Who's Who of Kinky Madams', and a special hot-line to take 'orders' for 'Big Dick Pills' guaranteed to double the penis size. (This last number received 23,000 calls in the first two days! Can you believe those wishful thinking men!)

Unfortunately, my hopes of banking a fortune from 0898 lines were short-lived. The director of International Telecom PLC – Mr John Gurney – refused to cough up my share of revenue. He claimed 'cash flow problems'. I later sued for breach of contract and got judgement against his company for £26,000. But I've not seen a penny. Others had claims against the company, too. (He was later charged by the Fraud Squad with two other defendants for conspiracy to defraud.) I wrote to my local Conservative MP – Sir Nicholas Scott – begging him to bring pressure to bear and help his needy constituent seek redress. He told me to contact the police. In desperation I turned to another Conservative politician – Peter Brooke, MP for Westminster South and the City of London, the area where International Telecom PLC's offices were based. He referred me back to Nicholas Scott. I felt that two prominent members of Parliament, elected to represent 'all' their constituents, had both turned their backs on a constituent robbed of a small fortune. This demonstrated – yet again – how whores are automatically denied equal civil, legal and economic rights.

MPs, police, tax inspectors and every other authoritative body to which I was expected to answer conveniently 'didn't notice' that I had been ripped off for some £75,000 (£30,000 worth of diamonds stolen at Acton, cheated out of £15,000 on Laxton Manor village green, £30,000 plus lost on 0898 lines). They didn't care or even sympathise, and this made me ask: 'What the hell am I getting for my taxes?' Nothing!

My political and legal friends pointed out that because BT had (mistakenly) recommended an unscrupulous, insolvent audio-text bureau, they should recognise responsibility for my loss. After all, before BT paid International Telecom PLC any of the substantial income generated from my lines, they had pocketed a fat percentage of the gross revenue as commission. I accused them of profiteering and demanded compensation, but they ignored me. This furthered my stance on 'better means of consumer redress' – another of my Corrective policies.

Disillusioned with 0898 lines, bureaucrats and 'the system', I spent my time sulking. Fortunately, when I sulk I doodle on reams of white paper, and these doodles developed into designs for bizarre costumes which in turn progressed into the launch of my 'Mistress Collection' – a line in kinky garments. My favourite was what I called the 'Rape Dress', a tattered frock which looked like it had been ripped off during a struggle. Word got round the grapevine, and I was inundated with requests to make unusual clothes and exotic underwear. For one eccentric lady I traipsed all the way to an East End leather importers to buy soft black kid, from which I created a beautifully grotesque black leather wedding dress covered with spiky silver studs and barbed wire. It took two weeks to make, and she was so pleased that she paid me double and then telephoned all her friends who subsequently placed bespoke orders and sent advance payments by registered post. Later I permitted a well-known magazine to publish this design. I had plenty of ideas for other fashions and dreamed big dreams of buying a shop to display them in. I rather fancied a brothel in the back room as well. This plan may still materialise!

I returned to the health farm to diet and improve the condition of my hair and nails. To alleviate any possibilities of boredom, I took along my computer, keyboards, recording equipment and video. I intended to generally shape up whilst planning tactics for the forthcoming London Council elections.

Politics was often on the agenda. It was frequently discussed in between massages, steam baths and yoga. On one occasion the Corrective, SDP and Conservative parties were jointly represented when Rosie Barnes, MP, Sir Charles Irving, MP (then in charge of catering at the House) and myself shared the same dining table, all naked under our robes. I often wondered how the tabloids would have reported such a scene! However, such sensationalism was unlikely because I had withheld my whereabouts from the media. I didn't want them pestering me for salacious sex scandals. A year previously the *Sun* had published an article about goings-on at a top health farm and I didn't want to be involved in any such notoriety.

When the Council elections came up I travelled back and forth between the health farm and Corrective headquarters (still based in the empty rooms above my dungeons). My clients said 'the best way into politics is at local-government level', so I took their advice and fielded three candidates, one for each ward in the borough of Kensington and Chelsea. No deposits are required for Council elections, so we were able to campaign on a shoestring budget. As a result, we hardly got a mention in the media and, as expected, we came last. But I was glad of the experience and it added another string to my political bow.

I have always found both sexes to be fascinated by my sexual knowledge, and keen to tell me their most intimate personal secrets. To them I was neutral, someone unshockable, someone 'safe' to confess to. Numerous sex-starved spinsters and, surprisingly enough, executive women too busy to cruise around 'singles' bars in the hopes of securing a well-hung one-night-stand, declared their willingness to hire a man to 'service' them. This prompted me to launch 'Studs', an idea I'd toyed with for several years, but had never put into operation. There was a gap in the market – which I could fill – by starting up a unique agency specialising in male escorts for randy women.

Over the years I had kept a number of female escorts on hand. There are a surprising number of 'girlfriends of convenience' needed in show business, for instance. On several occasions a well-known West End publicity agent, whose friends I'd often provided whores for, wanted a discreet young leggy brunette to act as a 'cover-up' (a fake lover) for a closet gay pop star. I had the ideal girl – Natasha. She know how to keep her mouth shut, and was a 'fag hag' (a women who hangs around gay men). The publicity agent paid her £2,000 and gave me a £300 'finder's fee', which of course he deducted from his client's account. It was essential that the star maintained his public image of being heterosexual, and Natasha had strict instructions to drool over him at various night-spots, making sure everyone noticed them.

As I knew a lot about supplying partners, Studs would be a lucrative extension of that. It wouldn't be difficult to find men either. Out of my thousands of clients I had made it my business to record the names and numbers of well-endowed ones who had shown willingness to 'pleasure' women in return for payment.

But in order to spread the word and make this venture viable, I needed another batch of 0898 sex lines to facilitate female clients seeking discreet information. They could simply dial up and listen. My 'Mistress Collection' had earned enough money to fund the advance rent required by BT, so I speedily signed contracts for thirty lines. With customers and advertising lined up, all I needed were the Studs themselves! I arranged to interview thirty-seven men. These Studs had only known me in a strict Mistress/submissive slave capacity, but now they had to be 'tested', and who better than me to make a decision? I awarded them marks out of ten: unfortunately, only four had the stamina worthy of employment. Fifteen poor performers scored five out of ten, eight incompetents rated two out of ten, and ten of them were utterly useless, scoring below zero! They screwed 'the armpit of my leg', thinking they were 'inside'!! Such attractive hunks too, what a waste of flesh!

My four prize Studs were all over 6 feet tall, good-looking, clean-shaven, with athletic builds and sporting well formed 8–9½ inch erections. I gave them mythological names: 'Thor', 'Adonis' 'Achilles' and 'Neptune'. It occurred to me that ads placed in sex mags would be a total waste of money because few women had the nerve to buy them. Regular women's mags didn't accept this kind of ad, so I had to rely on word of mouth and mailshots to selected women.

I drilled my Studs to pamper and cherish their clients, even if they were ugly old hags. The fees were £200 per hour from which I kept £50 commission; discounts were negotiated for longer sessions. For this, the female client was taken red roses and champagne, treated like a queen and made love to until she dropped from exhaustion. I made a rule: 'No orgasm – no charge.' Satisfaction was guaranteed. My Studs were experts, and I had a reputation to live up to – supplying only the best!

Studs was an instant success. Within the first ten days, my boys had repeatedly serviced eight women who responded to my mailshots. I had anticipated positive results – after all, mine was the only service tailored to this market – but what did surprise me was the unexpected types of women who wrote to me asking for my 'Studs' number. Quite a few satisfied ladies later wrote thanking me; one busy housewife said it was the best £200 she'd ever spent, and that it beat squandering similar amounts at beauty parlours where she received treatments far less beneficial!

Funnily enough, even this new strain of female client proved

Protesting with masked supporters before my 1987 tax hearing.

Lady of Laxton Manor with my own village green, perfect for a pillory.
Northamptonshire Evening Telegraph

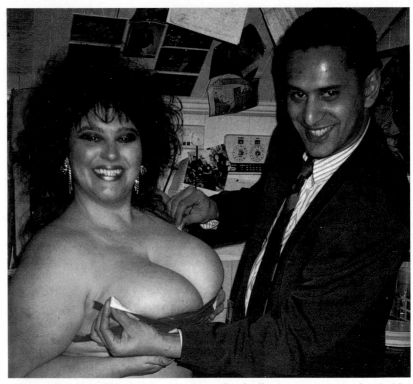

Above: With journalist Ray Levine. Six reels of sellotape were required to hold my 64″ KK tits in place for a tabloid photo shoot.

Left: With Jonathan Ross in the green room after appearing on his television show.

Below: Messing around with Ruby Wax while she filmed my kinky sex chambers.

Above: With Doc Cox in the make-up room before appearing on the 'James Whale Show'.

Above: Caught in the stampede as William Hague MP (Tory) wins the Richmond by-election, February 1989.

Below: Congratulating John Smith MP (Labour) as he wins the Vale of Glamorgan by-election, May 1989.

Below: Lobbying Ken Livingstone MP (Labour) during a demo in Hyde Park.

Above: Promising the electorate 'anything' if they *Vote Corrective*. *Jack Chapman*

Demonstrating 'Six of the Best' in front of the Conservative Club. Ribble Valley by-election, March 1991. *Lancashire Evening Telegraph*

useful in providing me with snippets of information to enhance my political efforts. One was a legal secretary, another a peer's daughter. Yet another had political connections, and she went out of her way to invite her friends and me to a dinner party which she put on especially so I could mingle with them. That night, my ears were like radar antennae, tuning into 'inside' political gossip which buzzed around the dinner table and over the ensuing rubber of bridge.

When the Liverpool Bootle by-election came up, I was still rejuvenating myself, so I asked another Party member to contest it. No-one had the guts to withstand being pulled to pieces by media hacks. I didn't blame them. It wasn't very nice trying to convey serious political points when all the time you knew the interviewer thought you were full of shit! Being a fringe candidate can be very demoralising and humilating, and my 'soldiers' needed time, just like I did, to look, listen and learn before putting themselves in the firing line. Bootle came and went, and we didn't stand which was a shame because we lost the chance to recruit more members (we always get some at by-elections).

I have visited many fat farms around the world, in America, Mexico and Europe, and I rate 'Safety Harbour Spa' in Tampa, Florida, as the best. But losing weight has always proved difficult. Extra pounds gained always go to my breasts, and the larger they get, the more my arms are pushed outwards. This can makes writing awkward and uncomfortable.

My consolation was knowing I wasn't alone in failure. I noticed the same dieters returning over and over again, all having regained weight they'd struggled to lose. Once thing that did surprise me was the number of 'slim' poseurs showing off designer jogging suits, and sexually permissive women seeking casual liaisons in the sauna or showers. This sort of thing quite repelled me. Even though I'm a hardened, unshockable purveyor of sexual services I *do* have my standards, and I'm appalled at the way 'straight' women, when away from home, let their hair down and 'give it away' to multiple casual strangers. There were two occasions when I noticed casual pick-ups 'having it off' under the jacuzzi bubbles – whilst I was sitting next to them! For me, this was a 'busman's holiday'. These establishments were like glorified brothels!

I was understandably extremely upset and angry when, after several weeks at one health farm, without prior notice, I was evicted by the management. They had, without my knowledge or permission, packed my belongings into dozens of black plastic dustbin sacks. I was told: 'We didn't know you were Miss Whiplash. Had we known we would have refused you admittance. We don't want a sex scandal.' I was outraged and demanded redress and compensation. Surely they had known who I was. I sent word to one of its directors that I would descend on his office with 200 whip-wielding prostitutes. Eventually I sued for breach of contract.

To cheer myself up I treated myself to a second-hand river cruiser. It was painted green, a big, wooden, six-berth monster with a diesel engine, formerly used as a Hoseason's hire boat on the Norfolk Broads. She was called 'Aliolin' (a mixture of Allison and Colin, the previous owners' names). I intended having a floating bordello, and wanted to re-name the boat 'Madam Thames' but didn't dare be so blatant on new ground. So I settled for the name 'Bit Iffey II' ('Bit Iffey I' had already been registered!). My new pseudonym was 'Madam Bullrush'. I rented a mooring along the bank of a deserted tributary at Chertsey, then I got a slave to move it to Bray Marina – more select, and full of enthusiasts angling off the decks of £250,000–£500,000 vessels with names like 'Gold Bullion' and 'Cops 'n' Robbers'. Needless to say, they all ended up on my mailshot databank. I sent out invitations: 'Your stiff rod will have more fun fishing at "Madam Bullrush's" floating brothel. Join our naughty girls every Sunday afternoon from 2 pm onwards.' A mobile phone number was given.

Cash was constantly needed to print Corrective Party material which was distributed by my NEC, members and supporters, so adding another business venture to my others seemed appropriate, particularly as I could mix it with my four favourite pastimes – sleeping, eating, counting money and sex (in that order)! Five of my favourite whores joined me during the summer weeks, and two submissive slaves (who were single, on the dole, and didn't need to account to anyone) were press-ganged into crewing. Naturally, they were kept in leg-irons, and regularly spanked.

Word went out and I enticed randy fishermen away from their quiet Sunday afternoon beers. There were numerous locks along the Thames. Making friends with an ex lock-master was a good move; he was a jolly old soul and as crooked as a nine-bob note. I named him 'Captain Penis'. He gave me a special lock key so we could open the locks automatically, which saved us the effort of opening them manually by turning a giant control wheel. Captain Penis became my 'punter-hunter' and was paid 10 per cent commission whenever he organised groups of men to attend sex orgies at £250 per head. We collected them from discreet pick-up points along the towpath. This was a luxury extension of when we 'girls' had gone round Hyde Park looking for customers.

He introduced us to all the local villains, many of whom were partial to a bit of slap and tickle. They 'hired' us to accompany them on an illicit sea trip to Puerto Banus in Malaga. Of course we were keen to provide 'ocean wave orgasms'. I ordered my two slaves (Dennis number 62 and Dennis number 24) to stay behind and paint my boat white in readiness for the forthcoming Henley Regatta, while we went to Spain.

I found life afloat relaxing and friendly; people waved and passed the time of day when they drifted by. Nothing like the rat-race of road travel where irate motorists constantly honk and cut you up. This was a new game and I liked it. Back at Bray Marina, I summoned eight other subservient males to participate in the Regatta, and us 'girls' tarted ourselves up in exotic rubber costumes. Our theme was 'Cleopatra's Slave Ship', and I combined various historical fetishes. I wore a black wig, long gold latex robes, heavy eye make-up and borrowed my friend's pet snake for my asp. My girls dressed in rubber and PVC period regalia, and between us we fulfilled the fantasies of an assortment of Dennises. They were chained below deck, together in two rows of five, using giant-sized knitting needles to respond to my commands:

'Row my galleon ship faster before I feed you to the lions. Row!'

My boat brothel continued to be very popular, particularly with discreet clients who had always wanted to visit me, but were scared of being seen visiting my house. These men responded to my mail-shots immediately. Some of them requested 'heavy bondage' so my kinky carpenter was called in to rustle up a set of stocks, a whipping post and a rack which he riveted to the deck. However, soon afterwards, a gale force 8 storm damaged the boat beyond repair. Winds wrenched the kinky gear from the deck – my stocks, rack and whipping post floated off down the Thames. 'Bit Iffey II' sank, sending my whips and fetish gear to a watery grave. The damage, set at £10,000, became too much of a liability, so I ended up giving my wreck to the Marina's salvage experts in lieu of mooring fees.

Back at Eardley Crescent, where several Corrective Party

members were kept busy dealing with the mounting administration, filing and political inquiries, an avalanche of paperwork was piling up from 'Castle Doom', Studs, Mistress Collection, Slutco and Rent-A-Fantasy. I wouldn't let my office staff touch it but the task was too daunting to do myself, so I persuaded 'Harold the Bookkeeper' to plough through the papers and prepare some ledgers for my accountant. His payment was straight sex, and it was through paying this debt that I discovered condoms with 'Nonoxynol 9' on them (a special ingredient reputed to kill the AIDS virus). In search of the safest and the best, I purchased every brand of condom available here and abroad, including one with a Union Jack on them, for patriotic clients. Some condoms had a lubricant with a paint-stripper effect which took off my nail varnish! (I shudder to think what it does to a uterus.) The condoms' only drawback was that they tasted vile for oral sex. However, they made me feel 'safe' enough to return full time to my House of Fetish and Fantasy and to earn some 'serious' money by taking back all may old 'straight sex' clients. I had expensive plans for the Corrective Party, so the more cash the better.

First, I did a few more alterations to the flat, this time making a 'court' room, in which to play 'law and order' games. Charlie (my minder) came back on the scene and I employed a new maid – Rose – who was so incredibly nosey that I couldn't resist pulling her leg. For a laugh I copied Harold the Bookkeeper's style and wrote up a set of 'fake books' which I accidentally-on-purpose left lying around, knowing full well that nosey Rosy would take a peek. These fake books had elaborate details of twenty girls each doing thirty to forty men a day, earning phenomenal sums of money. I even had a fake building society book with a million pounds deposited, and thousands of bogus shares. How I wished it was true! Charlie and I laughed our heads off, but this joke backfired when I was raided by two Customs and Excise VAT inspectors.

I had been paying VAT ever since 1989, when the VAT office first raided my establishment. The *Daily Mirror* ran the headline 'Ouch, VAT hurts' (referring to spanking). I registered under Section 8999, 'Other Services', as the sole proprietor of 'Lady of the Manor Fetish and Fantasy Enterprises' after being warned by everyone that the Customs and Excise were worse than the Inland Revenue! I had always paid my VAT on time, and I kept makeshift VAT records readily available for inspection. I didn't owe any VAT so I was confused as to why they had come.

However, this time they were more interested in examining my Corrective Party bank account. They suggested the donations were not really donations at all (which are exempt from VAT), but in fact money from prostitution (which isn't). I made them sit in the dungeon, on the bed-rack, as I answered a string of questions about my various business affairs. They wanted to examine my Corrective Party 'Treasury' files, but just like kinky clients required discretion, so did closet Correctives who'd donated anonymously. I refused to break confidences, and I was thoroughly pissed off when they searched my house, rooting through my cupboards and drawers. They didn't find my 'Treasury' records, but instead came across the fake brothel books and the building society book with the million-pound entry! Their eyes lit up like greedy kids in a sweet shop and despite my telling them the books were fake, they didn't believe me because they were 'too realistic'. After four hours they took away five carrier bags of paperwork for which they gave me a receipt. And as they departed, one said:

'Do you want to give us a cheque now?'

'Not likely!'

Being back in full-time prostitution meant the demand for my services was enormous. All my old regulars and been-befores, once notified of my return, wanted to come along in the first week. There were men everywhere! Some were so desperate that they accepted their service in the passage because the rooms were full. Others put hoods on and shared a room with another client (a submissive slave who wasn't allowed to object). I still kept my other businesses going and was working eighteen hours a day.

Let me tell you about my typical day. From the moment I get up, which is usually around 7 am, I sit at my word processor and type up the dream I had the night before whilst it's still fresh in my memory. I've always had erotic and sexually bizarre dreams. When I was a virgin schoolgirl I regularly dreamed I was being fucked by a green scaly demon with big red eyes, like bicycle reflectors. I record them in my 'dream book'. Sometimes I draw upon them for ideas when I'm doing my next chore – typing scripts for my 0898 sex lines. My mail arrives at 8 am, and I have a cup of tea and mull over the envelopes to see which ones I fancy opening. House of Commons or Royal letters are first, followed by envelopes with

BBC, ITN or SKY etc on them, then I open good quality stationery regardless of whom it's from. Letters from clients are next, then political inquiries, cheap stationery, illiterate letters and bills. In that order! I can't eat anything until I've been awake for four hours. I'm a late eater and like to sleep on a full stomach, which is the root of my weight problem.

My telephone lines start ringing from 8.30 am and they don't stop until 2 am. They are all answered by answering machines with a sexy tape inviting them to visit me at anytime between 11 am and 7 pm. (My hours change with my moods.)

I prefer my maid to clean the house, but sometimes she answers the phones to add a personal touch. However, this can be problematic because men who are regular time wasters with no intention of visiting repeatedly call and ask the same things. This blocks the line for genuine punters, and irritates me tremendously. At one point I asked my electronics expert friend to fix up a computer with facilities for voice prints, so I could match up the voice of nuisance callers. And on another occasion when I recognised the background noise of Earl's Court Tube, I sent Charlie across the road to find the caller and bring him to me. He frogmarched the nuisance from Earl's Court Station to my door, and my maid and I tried him in my courtroom. Charlie, who towered over the nuisance, made sure he complied. He confessed to phoning *all* my numbers over 2,000 times. Naturally, we found him guilty and he was fined £100 on the spot. Charlie made sure he paid up (he wrote a cheque), and he promised not to do it again. I couldn't believe it when he did! A month later his distinctive voice came down the line: 'Will you let me sniff your knickers? Does your hired 'gorilla' [Charlie] join in? You won't catch me this time. Ha ha!'

Throughout my day, in between clients, I work on my word processor logging my diary, updating my clientele, answering letters and making reports. I also run a kinky callback service, which is talking dirty to men on the phone. I charge them £30, which they pay by credit card, and they get fifteen minutes of utter verbal filth, completely uncensored. I have lots of regulars for this: some are heterosexuals, on the verge of bisexuality, guilty of cottaging (picking up men in public toilets) for the first time, and they need to confess; others are living in remote areas or are disabled. I do actually specialise in men with disabilities and special needs, and I even have a wheelchair and crutches in my surgery. On a few occasions I've visited such men in their nursing homes, and doing this made me realise that the disabled should be given surrogate sexual partners on the NHS. (This is another of my policies.)

At 8 pm I dine out with special clients or boyfriends or meet Corrective Party members to discuss new ideas. Then it's back to the word processor again, to key in the progress of my alternative businesses. In fact, spending so many hours in front of my VDU has given me blurry eyes and my doctor has told me to take a holiday. I've always been hyperactive, and having fingers in so many pies makes my mind feel like a computer on overload. In order to recharge my batteries, three out of every seven days I take off to a secret hideout in the country and live incognito as plain Mrs Average, in a 'normal' family life quite apart from my public persona.

When I want to 'get away from it all', I sneak off to Tetiaroa which is an atoll in French Polynesia, privately owned by Marlon Brando and where the original movie of *Mutiny on the Bounty* was filmed. Here it's back to nature, living naked in a palm-frond hut. No shops, no telephones, no newspapers and no tax inspectors.

As a rule, Thursdays are busiest for three reasons. Affluent men in top jobs tend to sow a few wild oats before being cooped up all weekend with their wives; working-class men have wage packets to treat themselves with; and new clients are enticed by massage ads carried by Thursday publications. One such recent Thursday was exceptionally busy, and many 'top-drawer' clients were booked in. I didn't even have time to open my post.

My first client, a pilot called 'Captain D', arrived at 8.30 am by appointment. After clearing Customs, he regularly stopped by for a three-hour bondage session which he said broke up the monotony of long-haul passenger flights. The second client, a passing stranger who fancied a quick bunk-up before going to work, turned up unexpectedly at 9 am. He'd seen my outside light on and thought I was open. (An exterior white light indicates a prostitute is available. Red lights are never used by discreet girls in residential areas. And a white light left on creates the illusion that regular tenants have forgotten to switch it off.) I had a little rhyme: 'Early to the door – busy for the whore', therefore I didn't want to bilk anyone because I was superstitious it would put the kybosh on my luck.

One after the other, regular clients trooped in: 'Ned', the shopkeeper, was in the dungeon; 'John', the electrician, was in the rubber room; 'M', the mercenary, who visited me in between fighting other people's wars, was in the torture chamber; 'Benny', an unemployed layabout who saved up his dole money for a visit, was in the nursery; 'Yew Tree', the chemist (so named because he's into home-made poisons, and yew leaves are toxic), was in the surgery; 'Rambo', an MP's son, was in the bedroom; 'Loot', who worked at the Royal Mint, was waiting in the spare toilet; and 'Daisy' a civil servant from MI6, was in the bathroom. Upstairs were two compliant 'domestic slaves' busily spring cleaning: 'Moneypenny', a Lloyds' name, was sweeping the floors, and 'Ruby', a civil servant from the Public Record Office, was washing down the paintwork.

By noon, 'M', who was having the 'total package' (a full day's kinky mixture of anything and everything – domination, bondage, correction, dressing up, etc, etc), wanted a rest from being stretched on the rack, so I demanded he made himself useful by stacking my mail on a silver tray – letters to one side, envelopes to the other. (I keep envelopes to check postmarks tally with where the writer claims to live. Correspondence I consider dangerous is handed to the police.)

When 5 o'clock came, multiple services had been administered to nineteen clients. I'd darted between rooms relieving them one by one and had completely forgotten about 'M' who'd been unattended in my office for some considerable time. I found him kneeling in the corner, chain-masturbating (one wank after another) over page 11 of my long-awaited Christie's catalogue which contained the 'Forman Archive of Crime and Punishment, including the Albert Pierrepoint [Britain's last hangman] Collection', due for auction in May 1992. This masochist's dream had arrived in the morning's post – twenty-four large glossy pages of medieval torture devices, including pictures of 18th-century metal man-traps, a steel chain slave's harness, a German iron body cage, an iron-hinged scold's bridle, and an 18th-century iron collar fitted with 6-inch exterior spikes. The *pièces de résistance* were an executioner's axe, an oak guillotine and a rope noose with the original hangman's record book. Page 14 was of particular interest to me, a photograph of a 1840s birching bench, used to punish male offenders in the West Midlands. At £2,500 I considered it extortionate, especially as it was no different from mine. Personally I thought my whipping trestle was a much better bargain at 90 per cent less (£250) and a unique history of punishing kinky MPs c. 1970–1990.

Until then I'd never considered the existence of a 'torture and bondage' collectors' market, and seeing restraint and punishment were my speciality, the idea of auctioning my own equipment crossed my mind as another means of raising capital to pay my tax debt. If Christie's guide prices (up to £30,000) hadn't been so high, I would have purchased a few authentic devices myself, as a treat to excite my slaves. Contrary to public opinion, perverts are rarely 'men in dirty raincoats'; kinks come in all shapes and sizes, and from all social classes. Having serviced so many, I wasn't at all surprised that someone as masculine as 'M' had a perverse sexual quirk. He reminded me of Jake, only 'M' worked for an army and Jake worked for the underworld. I despise violence (except consensual S&M sex games), but 'M' justified his work by saying, 'I kill the country's enemy'. Jake used to say, 'I kill anybody's enemy'. Like most kinks, 'M' confessed a desire to 'experience what it's like on the other side of the fence'. He was a particular favourite of mine, and extremely useful if ever anyone upset me. After all, who wants to face a mercenary soldier avenging his wronged Mistress!

During the run-up to the auction, I teased dozens of regulars with the catalogue. The idea of 'real' slavery aroused them. On the day, fifteen clients posed as 'pseudo-bidders' and managed to join me at Christie's, just to ogle at and touch the items. They all used the same ruse, large newspapers held in front of their groins in order to hide bulging erections. And when I noticed strangers doing the same thing, I wondered if they too were kinks. Never one to miss an opportunity, I had taken calling cards and kinky photographs along, just in case prospective customers were to be found.

My clients dotted themselves amidst the audience, keeping their distance from me in case Press photographers snapped them. I sat in the back row, observing who bid for what. And I laughed when a female bid, knowing my clients were fantasising she was a Mistress. When the auction ended, I waited outside and introduced myself to several successful male bidders, inviting them to come and see 'my' collection. Some were disinterested, claiming their attendance was purely on behalf of a client, but others enthused over colour photos of my torture chamber and promised to give me a call.

I continue to be an eccentric extrovert, keen to attain the unattainable, and when the joint British/Russian 'Juno' space mission advertised for an astronaut, I couldn't resist applying. I knew there was no way I'd be accepted, so for a laugh I submitted a

C.V.

Name: Lindi St. Clair BSc (Brothels Serving the Community)

Address: 58, Eardley Crescent, London, SW5 9JZ

D.O.B.: 1.1.60

(Sorry, I lie about my age)

Education:

International Vice School, Paris, France.
(Courtesan Class of 73).

Qualifications Passed with Honours:

Missionary Position	Rent Boy Liaison	Stiletto Worship	Sex Slave Humility
Doggy Fashion	Lesbianism	Strict Nanny Discipline	Transvestism
Knee Trembler	Water Sports	Mistress Dominance	Leather Bondage
64"KK Smothering	Gang Bangs	Sado Masochism	Rubber Nurse Castration
Deep Throat	Flogging	Verbal Telephone Sex	Regression to Babyism
Body Massage	Code of Ethics	Naughty Boy Caning	Code of Silence

All the above qualifications are accepted internationally

Employment Record:

1974–1975: Madame Guillotine's Bordello, Paris, France
1975–1976: Charlotte's Harlots, Las Vegas, USA
1976–1977: Floating Lesbian Brothel, Isle of Lesbos, Aegean Sea
1977–1978: Alligator Swamp Cat House, Jefferson County, Louisiana
1978–1979: House of Condoms, Earl's Court, London
1979–1980: Personal Services Ltd., Earl's Court, London
1980–1982: Coconut Love Hut, Tetiaroa, French Polynesia
1982–1983: Falklands Secret Brothel, Shag Rocks, South Georgia
1983–1984: Mustang Chicken Ranch, Nevada Desert, USA
1984–1985: Miner's Shafting Shack, Kalgoorlie, Western Australia
1985–1987: Nookie Nest, Wan Chi, Hong Kong
1987–1989: Fetish Torture Chamber, Earl's Court, London
1989–1990: Madam Kinky's Slave Farm, Ixtapan Hills, Mexico
1990–1992: Slutco UK Sex Dungeon, Earl's Court, London

Special Skills:

Ability to keep 135,365 men exceedingly 'happy' worldwide, including 52 British Lords and 204 British MPs. I practise 'safe data' capture, your data is secure with me.

Security:

I have been thoroughly vetted by the security services. I have kept them all 'satisfied' over a number of years. I make 'Special Branch' special.

humorous application along with a nude photo. I introduced myself as Lindi St Clair, BSC (Brothels Serving the Community), with qualifications listed as 'harness making' – essential to keep astronauts in their seats – and 'vast sexual experience' – essential for assessing inter-planetary mating habits. My knowledge of languages was listed as French (the code word for oral sex), and previous experience included 'experiments involving the depths of human endurance' – which of course was my S&M torture services. My answer to 'why I was most suited for the position' was 'I'm experienced in all "positions" including "missionary", "doggy fashion" and "knee trembler". My clients at NASA agree I am the perfect choice to relieve all sticky situations and would be ideal for stimulating crew morale.' I was delighted to get a personal reply from the mission's captain: 'Thank you for your most interesting application. I will keep your details should any future position arise.' I didn't get the photograph back . . .

Recently I spotted an advertisement in *The Times* for a temporary secretary for a Tory MP. I sent in a similar CV, but he didn't reply!

Self-made humorous interjections are the key to my success. Whenever situations get difficult, I look for the funny side of things and have a good laugh. And given the trials and tribulations I've encountered, compared to 'straight' women of my age, I seem to have significantly less wrinkles. I attribute this to ample laughter, sleep and orgasms!

12

Sexual Politics

In the 1992 General Election, the Corrective Party was defeated by lack of time to submit multiple nominations, lack of money, and lack of nerve on the part of quite a few candidates who had promised to promote civil liberties, social justice, animal rights and equal opportunities. Gay candidates committed to campaign against homophobic laws, like Section 28 and Clause 25, chickened out at the last moment. Those into legalising cannabis suddenly disappeared through fear of being busted. And others who were sexually deviant let me down out of spite, because I rejected their sexual advances.

Ardent supporters had regularly donated towards campaign funds, but there wasn't enough to pay £25,000 for fifty candidates' deposits, plus another £100,000 to publish and fold 3 million election leaflets. Furthermore, the fancy five-minute election broadcast I wanted cost £250,000 (£50,000 per minute). Ken Russell rallied to the cause and offered to direct it free of charge. His producer, Ronaldo Vasconcellos, waived his fee, and they 'called in some favours' which reduced the cost to £35,000, but it still exceeded our budget.

What pissed me off most were the hours of wasted time and energy co-ordinating my campaign: not dissimilar to an army general manoeuvring soldiers into 'attack mode'. I had spent months standing in front of a giant constituency map plotting tactics with little pink pins, marking my soldiers' positions. I had been prepared to subsidise the Corrective Party campaign from my prostitution earnings, but the taxman's demands superseded these ambitions.

On 9 April, the day of the election, I telephoned all my clients and boyfriends who were MPs or parliamentary candidates, and left good-luck messages on their answering machines. Then, from 11 pm until 8 am the following morning, I sat glued to the TV studying what was happening in order to glean ideas for next time around. Most important to me was to gauge how much media coverage the small parties received. My observations relating to the Natural Law Party – £155,000 in lost deposits for the 64,000 votes gained, 0.2 per cent of the total cast, and hardly any television coverage – made me realise that they hadn't had full value. It is obvious that in a General Election, the main parties are allowed to dominate, and that there was more mileage for small or fringe parties in a by-election.

I must confess that my own support was divided. I've loved men in all three main parties and wished my clients and boyfriends could team up in one super party – all on the same side!

I was shocked that all the winners of the by-elections I had contested were now out again, and amused that both Glenys and Norma chose to wear Corrective Party pink. John Major went up in my estimation when I saw him all macho, dragging Norma away from the media. Now I'm really confused as to which politician to admire the most!

The election results were a milestone in my life, and gave me cause for personal reflection. I had ignored the 1979 and 1985 elections just like millions of other abstainers who say: 'MPs are full of shit, they're just out for what they can get.' This most recent one was the first during which I'd been politically conscious; people I counted as friends had participated. I watched with pride as some of my 'boyfriends' won their seats for the first time. But a lump formed in my throat when others dear to me were voted out of office.

All this was quite an achievement for a cheeky schoolgirl who didn't realise that France would be only the beginning of her travels; that the original quest for the Countess would lead to discovering so many more places. I've come a long way from life in the gutter, lice in my hair, and sleeping in rubbish tips.

I reckon it was the combination of three particular qualities which enabled me to climb to the top of my vocation: I had my own money from the start; I was a good actress; and I was willing to go whichever way the wind blew. The influence of two people also stayed with me. Jake taught me the wisdom of silence: 'See everything, hear everything, say nothing.' And Madame's advice went a long way to ensure the success of my brothels: 'Remember, a customer is always right even if he's wrong.' Through them I learned enough to become a woman of property off my own bat (or back!).

In order not to forget my early days, I recently rescued one of the old 'K5' red telephone boxes in which I once plied my trade. It stands in my front garden, a local landmark, freely available for any whore wishing to affix her stickers on its windows.

A media broadsheet recently labelled me an 'Elder Stateswoman' on the subject of prostitution. This was somewhat disconcerting. However, as I've now promoted the importance of legalising prostitution for some twenty years, I suppose they are right. Since then, the *Independent* has come up with the more appropriate 'Evergreen Lindi', which I must confess I prefer. The way in which I can best accomplish the legalising of prostitution is to become an MP. If I do, I'll be unique. There would be no need for anyone to dig up dirt, as I'm totally honest about what I have been. And I couldn't be bribed: I've had pots of cash, diamonds, minks, land etc. I'm no longer materialistic. When you've had it, been there, done that – there's no lure. Nowadays, I'm quite happy to settle for a cheese sandwich, a cup of tea and watching the soaps on television.

I have often been asked in interviews what advice I would give to a young girl embarking on prostitution. If I am expected to offer discouragement they are in for a surprise. I believe in financial autonomy, freedom of choice and supply and demand. The argument that legalised brothels would attract more girls into the profession is a favourite amongst bigots and moralists, and I do not accept it at all. Having busily researched prostitution at first hand, since I was thirteen years old, I have proved that only certain types of girls, with a particular chemical make-up, enter the trade. I can accept the argument that some young no-hopers drift into prostitution through poverty and desperation, but these girls are not virgins and are sexually permissive to begin with. I back up my findings by comparing these girls to others who are in the same situation, but have a different chemical make-up. They're the ones who say, 'I would rather die than sell my body,' and they get by doing menial jobs or begging or stealing. They would never prostitute themselves because they are 'not that type'. (Throughout this book, I have referred to women prostitutes, but I fully recognise that this trade involves both male and female workers – as the gay lobby so frequently remind me!)

Whores who drift into seedy red-light areas rarely have any sex education, and certainly no enthusiasm for prosperity. If they worked 'straight' they would remain at the bottom; for example, they'd forever 'fill shelves' with no ambition to climb up the promotional ladder to management level. These whores hate their work, but they hate conventional jobs even more! A significant number of no-hopers who have been abused in childhood turn to alcohol and drugs, then get saddled with pimps who exploit and brutalise them. They would rather have a pimp on hand to protect them from dangerous punters than have no-one to protect them at all. They live a foul, sordid, anonymous life in the gutter, from which they rarely escape.

Then there is a percentage of sensible young whores who drift into the game; avoid pimps and drugs; save their money and drift back out again.

On the other side of the coin are girls like me, sexually aware, intelligent, enterprising, extrovert and nymphomaniac, who are in their element counting money and sleeping with strangers. Rather than waste our skills working 'straight' for somebody else, or be the local 'pub slag' dropping our knickers for a few gin and tonics (there's one in every pub), we make an informed choice to kill two birds with one stone and sell sex.

I reckon there could be as many as two million prostitutes in Britain. These include hard-core professionals and part-time amateurs; the low-paid and students who subsidise their budgets with a few clients; bored housewives seeking sexual fulfilment; and even daughters of the aristocracy who see random clients for devilment. They all inhabit a secret, hidden environment about which the media and authorities can only speculate. If prostitution were legalised and a 'sudden' influx of whores registered themselves, it wouldn't mean these girls had been attracted into the business – they were already there! The 'influx' would simply mean that prostitutes had come 'out of the closet' and emerged from the black economy.

To new would-be whores I suggest that they save their cash and get off the streets as quickly as possible. They should avoid pimps because no matter how romantic, caring or protective he appears, he will eventually make you his prisoner. The primary rules of the game are, always insist on a condom being used, and work with a friend. Never be entirely alone with a punter, as you never know which one is a murderer. This is why the brothel law should be amended. It is ridiculous that under today's law, one prostitute working alone within premises is legal, but if you add another girl, it constitutes a brothel and is illegal. (All other workers and traders are allowed to share premises. Only prostitutes are excluded.) It also means that prostitutes are therefore prevented from protecting their lives!

Another incongruity is the illegality of prostitutes advertising, touting or soliciting clients. How therefore can they ply their trade? It's like saying 'You can have a car, you can drive it, but you can't have petrol!'

Prostitutes are denied equal civil, economic and legal rights, and are the only workers excluded from the Government's Health and Safety Act. This became very obvious with Chris's death. I had warned the police there were threats to kill her, and if they had listened, she would still be alive today. Two other close friends have been murdered. Julie should have been safe, as she had a friend with her when she picked up a punter in Park Lane. However, the man suddenly pulled out a gun and she was shot. (Her friend managed to escape.) Sharon, one of my escorts, who lived round the corner from me, was strangled by a client. (It was rumoured he was a VAT inspector!) Around the same time in Earl's Court a client tried to strangle Lucy, but she escaped; and only because her pimp was in the next room did the murder attempt on Jackie fail. The police approached me, suspecting a serial killer, and I was whisked off to the scene of the crime feeling like 'Columbo' as I discussed possible motives.

Television news programmes consulted me: 'What's the general feeling amongst the prostitutes?'

'Anger and contempt for a Government that does nothing to protect them!'

Sharon's murder was neither pursued very vigorously nor resolved, and in 1991 the Corrective Party demonstrated against this poor treatment. We wanted 'Perestroika and Glasnost for sexuality'; the 'Berlin Wall of prudery' had to come down. Parliament was in summer recess, so twenty of us went to the Home Office with placards saying:

'MPs lie in the sun
Prostitutes lay in the morgue.'

Unfortunately, this was the day Gorbachev was pushed out, so we didn't get any publicity. An underling was sent down to receive our letter of protest. We were dismissed, with not even an acknowledgment from the Home Secretary to whom it was addressed. This was grossly unfair. When pit bull terriers attacked, Kenneth Baker bent over backwards to bring in emergency legislation. 'Dangerous dogs' were muzzled, and he gave the same dedication to 'joyriding'.

Back in the seventies, the Yorkshire Ripper epitomised how easy it was for killers to target prostitutes, since when hundreds of isolated prostitutes have been butchered, and nothing has been done. Prostitution has proved dangerous and fatal countless times. The authorities' indifference has forced many sex workers to take matters into their own hands. Some carry illegal firearms, others stock up with CS gas smuggled in from Europe. I fully support their view that it is better to risk conviction for firearms than be helpless at the hands of a psychopathic killer.

It is this State indifference to the fate of prostitutes that encourages attackers and murderers to target them because they believe there is less chance of police investigation, and that they will therefore more easily elude capture and prosecution. But there is a far greater risk to the public than is presently assumed. These attackers can very easily confuse prostitutes with non-prostitutes, and when stirred up by 'Ripper' fantasies, *any* target will suffice.

Despite this, the subject obviously remains too unsavoury for the Home Affairs Select Committee to debate. Given the statistics of danger, death and disease, I would have thought it is in the public interest for Virginia Bottomley to at least discuss the pros and cons of legalising brothels. To date she has shown little sympathy. I have written to her suggesting she consider my evidence. This shouldn't involve her or any other Government department in too much work. When pro-prostitution pressure groups use the phrase 'legalise prostitution and brothels', this does not imply State control; prostitutes should just be allowed *by law* to organise their own business affairs, without interference. Obviously they would work to a code of ethics, confidentiality and practice as doctors, bankers and lawyers do.

If prostitution were decriminalised, small collectives would work together within safe, discreet, private premises. This would minimise danger and save on police resources currently deployed convicting vice girls. As an example of this waste of time, every night, like clockwork, the Vice Squad cruise around Shepherd's Market in London, frequently stopping to take prostitutes off to be charged. They are bailed out and fined £25 upwards at court the following morning. This is exactly the same as a pimp rounding up his girls and taking them off to pay 'rent' for their 'pitch'. The safety inherent in girls working together in 'collectives' would also save the State massive funds in murder investigations and murder trials.

The best locations for these legal brothels would be self-contained flats over shops in non-residential busy shopping precincts where clients could simply slip inside unnoticed amongst crowds of shoppers. 'Toleration zones' are isolated carparks or other waste land where punters and whores can park up for business. But these guarantee no protection against attackers and would create a 'leper colony' type atmosphere. Self-respecting whores would resent a 'State-run meat-market' and discreet punters wouldn't risk being spotted heading in that direction. Prior to the General Election some Tory candidates publicly expressed interest in British 'toleration zones', but they talked out of their backsides. Like other non-prostitutes who recommend changes, they've spent five minutes in Amsterdam and think they know all the answers!

Some say that decriminalising prostitution would mean a free-for-all for pimps to spring up everywhere and force girls on to the game. This is utter nonsense, and in any event there are laws concerning kidnap and demanding money with menaces laws which amply cover such exploitation.

Mandatory health-checks wouldn't eradicate the spread of disease, but they would certainly minimise it. And there are other health aspects to consider. If a man fell over in a shop and broke his leg, he could sue. But there's no redress if a client is robbed by a pimp, or gets syphilis or HIV during his service. And over thirty prostitutes known to me have died of AIDS. One girl was a virgin! She had a deformed vagina and never did intercourse. Her speciality was 'bareback deep throat' (fellatio without a condom) and for hygiene she gargled with antiseptic mouthwash and vigorously brushed her teeth in between clients. She got infected with HIV through having bleeding gums.

It is vital that the Government sets up a 'Prostitute Health Fund', to which every prostitute would contribute over the years (like a pension fund). When prostitutes got diseased they could cease work and receive a substantial wage from this Health Fund. This is the only way to prevent diseased prostitutes from spreading infection. No prostitute sick with HIV or with painful, infected genitals wants to sell sex, she only continues working to maintain her standard of living. This is why the special fund is so essential.

Promising support came in April 1992. With the approval of the Right Rev. David Shepherd, head of the Church of England's Board on Social Responsibility, the Mothers' Union, a respectable women's organisation, invited a debate among their members which meant 250,000 upstanding ladies discussing the possibilities of legal brothels, something I have been advocating for years. The editor of their magazine, *Home and Family*, believed 'the debate is relevant because of the effect AIDs has and will continue to have on family life unless more is done to control it.'

This announcement brought a flurry of objections from figures like Mary Whitehouse. I was called in to address Sky News, dozens of local radio stations and the World Service. I debated with representatives from the Mothers' Union and a similar organisation, the Josephine Butler Society. But like Mary Whitehouse, they were elderly women who had spent their adolescence and sexually active years in another era. How could they possibly speak for today's sexuality? Each programme was live, leaving me only a few minutes to get my message across. Fortunately, I am now rehearsed in my lines; after all I've been broadcasting the same argument for years.

Requests constantly arrive from the media for information on prostitution. Certain journalists have leaked secret Government reports to me and sought my views. In 1991 'The Heart of the Matter' with Joan Bakewell gave the subject a sympathetic hearing. An enthusiastic Reverend joined in and supported the cause: 'In the light of AIDS, it is more Christianly ethical to legalise and control prostitution, rather than the supposedly Christian view to eradicate it. Prostitution is a healing therapy, and anything which heals must have a holy spirit.' But I think perhaps the Rev. had an ulterior motive: he borrowed my sex magazines and has not returned them yet!

Another prominent man who 'went public' to support positive changes in the sex laws was the writer and barrister Francis Bennion. He was an ex-Parliamentary draftsman who'd responded to my public appeal. I'd hoped he would draft my 'Sexual Services Bill', but nothing materialised.

Certain elements of the media have treated me badly; journalists have picked my brains and filched my findings, passing them off as their own, without so much as a thank-you. TV presenters have gleaned otherwise unavailable information and dumped me at the last minute. I now have a personal black-list of programmes on which I refuse to appear. But gradually I am becoming the recipient of profuse apologies. Those who have previously dismissed me, invariably need to consult me because I am their only reliable source. My list gets shorter as they grovel to get back into my favour!

I was delighted, as a follow-up to the Mothers' Union announcement, that a spokesman for the Catholic Church in England and Wales admitted they held a watching brief: 'If the discussion reveals new insights we will debate the subject.' Unfortunately, previous experiences have left me feeling pessimistic.

In August 1991, I commissioned a MORI poll which proved that, without any prior public debate, already 55 per cent of the population supported new legislation. From 148 sampling points throughout Britain, 2,000 people aged 15 plus from all social levels were asked, 'On balance, would you support or oppose small, discreet, legal brothels?' Only 12 per cent were against and 33 per cent didn't know. The most support came from professional men in the South. However, these significant findings were not even acknowledged by the Government.

Earlier on, in January 1991, I had participated in the BBC programme 'People in the News', and 75 per cent of viewers called in to support legalised prostitution. The subsequent questioning of the reliability of opinion polls after the General Election led me to believe my MORI poll support could have been more. People may have been too shy to admit their true feelings to a pollster. This was borne out by a response in 'Question Time', the weekend of 24 April 1992, which related to the Mothers' Union debate. Jonathan Dimbleby took a snap vote from the audience regarding legal brothels, and discovered an overwhelming proportion in favour.

Several establishment figures have recognised my knowledge on the subject and that what I am saying makes sense. In November 1991, the House of Commons requested information on brothels as they had nothing for members' reference. My Corrective Party

'Prostitution Report' – a compilation of otherwise unavailable information on statistics, facts, habits and the population of prostitutes, Madams, clients and pimps worldwide – now proudly sits in their library. (I update it occasionally.) In February 1992, the Birmingham Vice Squad came to see me for some answers on how to deal with problems in their own area. Lord Denning has sent students researching the legalisation of prostitution to my door. One wrote a very favourable article in the Cambridge Michaelmas *Political Review*. Judge Pickles and I have debated on the same side on television.

Recently I addressed an international MENSA conference called 'Power, Sex and Money', held at Queen's College, Cambridge. An article about this appeared in the late lamented *Punch*. The writer said I made my audience realise that the Corrective Party had a serious intent. She may well have been flippant when she said: 'She made life on the game seem easy, with men faithfully following prostitutes around brothels as their wives kept up with favourite hairdressers.' (However, she was closer to the truth than she realised in coupling men, their wives and prostitutes, as it is a known fact among us that Christmas is our best time of the year: men bring their wives into the West End for Christmas shopping, and go off to give themselves a seasonal treat in a prostitute's flat!)

Another publication, *The Police Review*, used me as a peg to hang a story on, when I bought some rock and roll memorabilia – a cheque made out to the Inland Revenue and signed by John Lennon. They published my picture and listed various statistics on prostitution. In 1986 in England and Wales, 7,448 women were fined a total of £286,625 for soliciting and in the same year, 211 women were imprisoned for fine default in prostitution offences. That added up to nearly 8,000 women in one year. Here was a classic illustration of the waste of public money involved in pursuing these women – money which could have been put to far better use. How can I ever give up on pressing for the decriminalisation of prostitution when such anomalies exist?

Then I was invited to speak at the Esher College of Further Education, which was reminiscent of the grammar school I had addressed during the Ribble Valley by-election. A Corrective Party leaflet on every chair wasn't nearly enough for the crowd that packed the hall. Some were clinging to the plush curtains for support, and the windows steamed up. The questions were far-ranging: how would I set up a brothel; several were as interested in legalising cannabis as sex; but one wanted to know what the age limit would be on brothel employees. These were young, inquiring liberal minds – tomorrow's voters – and they were satisfied with my answers.

I am forced to turn down hundreds of invitations which flood into my cramped Corrective Party headquarters. Far-flung universities, schools and hospitals seem to think I can afford the time and expense to address them without any consideration of a fee. Whilst I am anxious to get my message across, I also have to earn a living. However, if it's within a 4-mile radius, and it's charitable or worthwhile, I will make an exception. Recently, Charing Cross Hospital paid me £30 (a tenth of my earnings for the same time-slot) to address six nurses from the sexually transmitted disease clinic on how prostitutes cope with disease and danger.

My reasons for forming the Corrective Party are as strong as ever. I have policies on all issues, to correct the entire system with radical reforms and new ideas, but the main aim, in which I have a vested interest, is to promote positive alternatives in the sex laws. I have to keep hammering that home. I am hoping that brothels will be legal in Britain by 1997, but William Hill, the bookmakers, refused to take odds on it.

MPs are coming closer to admitting in public, even if not in the House, that new legislation would be beneficial. Recently, a Labour back-bencher who sided with me on a television programme invited me to the Commons for a drink. I was in a mischievous mood and tried bartering with him for a spare roll of House of Commons' wallpaper. The giant portcullis pattern would have looked a treat in my House of Fetish and Fantasy; a Parliamentary seal of approval. But I blew my opportunity to discuss more serious matters. When my host was called away to the telephone, I got bored waiting so I polished off a few too many glasses of champagne. This led to me making outrageous remarks to Ann Widdecombe, Parliamentary Under Secretary for Social Security. I did later apologise with an enormous basket of flowers, but she refused to accept it because she disapproved of the source of my income. (Pity the Collector of Taxes isn't so fussy – he doesn't seem to mind where it comes from, he just wants it!)

Several MPs enjoying a quiet drink looked worried that I might say something about *their* sexual habits! Then I drifted into another Commons bar and flirted around the assembled company, cheekily affixing my 'Ticket to Ride' stickers (complimentary brothel passes) on their wine glasses. I had fun teasing MPs present that in the event of the Corrective Party withdrawing from the next Election I would urge my members and supporters to vote for them. They began to compete amongst themselves as to who would justify the extra votes.

There were Tories saying, 'The Correctives are voting for us!'

Labour was arguing back, 'No, it's us!'

What none of them realised was my continuing soft spot for the Lib Dems. I had befriended many of them during by-elections and had even exchanged letters with Paddy Ashdown on certain political matters. And it was in Paddy Ashdown's favour that I finally considered committing the ultimate indiscretion.

The years of constant injustice pushed me over the edge. Prostitutes were still being murdered willy-nilly all over the country and the Government's attitude to my calls for action hadn't changed. 'She's only a whore it doesn't matter.' Acting on impulse, prompted by anger and frustration, I wrote to Paddy Ashdown offering him my '*Dirt File*'. This contains times, dates and places, with corroborating photographs and videos of Labour and Conservative MPs who frequent prostitutes. I've never been known to break a confidence before and I am conditioned to regard what takes place between a prostitute and a client as sacred. It's just as well that Paddy rejected this offer, because I didn't really want him to 'tell on my boys'.

My conditions would have been a safe Lib Dem seat. Just imagine if Paddy had accepted! My '*Dirt File*' contained enough evidence to disgrace a significant number of the Government and Opposition out of office. There could have been a landslide Lib Dem victory, Paddy Ashdown could have been Prime Minister, and I could have been 'Minister of Brothels'!

Instead my tax nightmare has come true and I am finally forced to face the music. Recently I had a meeting with my accountant Dennis Gilson, who had cleverly retained the service of the original 'enemy' tax inspector who had toured my brothel back in the early eighties. He had left the Civil Service and was now available to advise clients like me who had once been on the receiving end of his ruthless taxation decisions.

I hadn't seen Dennis for years; immediately I noticed his prosperity. His former cramped consultancy had spread into the adjoining building. The one thing that hadn't changed was his annoying habit of nagging someone on the phone whilst punctual clients waited outside his door. The ex-tax inspector turned up a few moments later and shook my hand with such force my fingers smarted. It turned me on – I love strong men! He was typically grey: the stereotype professional with regulation glasses, overcoat and briefcase; the sort that commutes from the City to suburbia. Being too business-like to waste time, he began advising me there and then – in the passage!

Dennis, a minuscule man of about five foot, finally hung up the phone and beckoned us into his office. His enormous oak desk, much bigger than he was, dominated the room. My tax liability had escalated into a minefield of debt, not far short of £200,000. The figure didn't seem quite so alarming when he said it quickly, but written down – wow! All those zeros! Mr Pinkney of the Inland Revenue Enforcement Office in Worthing was not prepared to make any deals or take payment by instalments. He had made it clear: 'Pay up immediately, or I'll bankrupt you.' Things looked grim and I felt like a damsel in distress with my knight in a neat grey suit fighting to rescue me.

My one fear has always been bankruptcy which would debar me from standing for Parliament. I also dread the thought that, at my time of life, I should be reduced to a bag lady with nothing left. Would I really have to descend from the bricks and mortar of my opulent House of Fetish and Fantasy to a makeshift dwelling of brown corrugated packaging on the cold pavements of Charing Cross or Waterloo? Would I have to swap a satin-covered king-sized feather bed for a mattress of yesterday's newspapers, from counting customers in minks, cars, jewels and votes, to counting them in sandwiches, bags of chips or entry to the public baths? As a Cardboard City courtesan inside my box I'd stick red cellophane sweet wrappers over the white beam of a cheap torch, and in a sleazy glow sell sex to tramps at 25 pence a time.

In the taxi home from the accountant's, I reminded myself that things could be worse – just imagine, for instance, being a laboratory monkey born to a living hell suffering vivisection experiments. I slouched back in the seat and totted up what I could sell to raise capital. There was my title, the 'Lordship of Laxton Manor', and some ghoulish artefacts I'd bought from Christie's, like Dr Crippen's last letter written from his death cell, instructing solicitors to dispose of his belongings. I also had execution warrants signed by Louis XIV and a set of 1723 Newgate prison records listing Jonathan Wilde, 'the thief taker', and eighteen highwaymen. These goodies had been displayed on my torture chamber walls to heighten clients' fantasies but they were hardly enough to keep Mr Pinkney off my back.

Raising cash on the brothel property proved impossible. Financiers have always considered prostitutes a 'bad risk', and offer rock-bottom funds at premium-rate interest. Selling up was also a non-starter – who wants to live in a brothel! Only developers would be interested, at a fraction of the true value.

Luckily I'm a resilient person, and as bankruptcy looms, I'm all set for the wind to blow me in another direction. Needless to say, I am totally stunned at what must be the biggest irony of all time. Criminalised for prostitution. Simultaneously taxed. And my brothel seized in lieu of revenue. *I've always said the State was a pimp!*

Recently I had a vivid dream, and it was promptly recorded in my dream book. I was made bankrupt and the Official Receiver obtained a court order to evict me and auction my assets. As usual, to let the world witness British hypocrisy at its best, I tipped off the media who turned up in droves to watch the bailiffs physically put a brothel-keeper out on the streets. This was a world first! Under bankruptcy law, one's entire estate is confiscated and sold to pay off debts. However, the tools of one's trade are exempt, so they could not take my kinky sex equipment.

Accompanied by police escorts and a locksmith who sawed through my iron-barred security gate, four burly bailiffs forced an entry, breaking down the heavy medieval oak door as I cursed them through the window. In a desperate attempt to remain, I chained myself to the dungeon wall, but the bastards had bolt cutters and snapped the chains in an instant. They dragged me out, up the basement steps, and ruthlessly tossed me on to the pavement. So there I was, the tart with a heart, in fishnet stockings, stiletto boots, a topless black PVC dress, angrily waving my leather bullwhip. Rendered homeless and brothel-less by a bigoted Government, I was outraged.

TV crews and photographers busily recorded the scoop. My rack, stocks, whipping post, pillory, hangman's gallows, gibbet, punishment cage, leather and rubber bondage gear, whips, canes, handcuffs, costumes, dildos, vibrators, condoms and the beds were dumped in the street next to me.

That was only a dream. Could it become a reality? One thing for sure is that I will never be short of a bed. Of my 5,037 'regulars', 12,241 'been befores', 225 'boyfriends' and 23,958 'strangers', I'm sure plenty will rally to the cause. Alternatively, I could always sleep in my pink Range Rover. It has a mattress in the back. I still have the means of earning a living.

I've made and lost many fortunes in my time, and this is yet another part of my personal game of Monopoly. So far I've gone round the board five times, bought Mayfair, collected rents, gone to jail; now I must reverse ten squares back, lose a 'go', and wait until I throw a double six.

But it will happen: 'Where there's a willy, there's a way!'

Ode to Hypocrites

They say my life is full of trash
But still they tax my dirty cash
In decadence they say I dwell
Won't go to heaven, just to hell

Those who never give me thanks
Seem happy selling guns and tanks
To them I'm just a dirty whore
Cos I make love, whilst they make war!

Lindi St. Clair

If you would like to support the Corrective Party, please send a stamped addressed envelope for details to:

Corrective Party,
58 Eardley Crescent,
London, SW5 9JZ